WHAT HAPPENS WHEN I DIE?

a promise *of* the afterlife

BRIAN C. STILLER

What Happens When I Die? : a Promise of the Afterlife

Copyright ©2012 Brian C Stiller
All rights reserved
Printed in Canada
International Standard Book Number: 978-1-894860-43-7

Published by:
Castle Quay Books
1307 Wharf Street, Pickering, Ontario, L1W 1A5
Tel: (416) 573-3249
E-mail: info@castlequaybooks.com
www.castlequaybooks.com

Cover design by Cindy Thompson
Printed at Essence Printing, Belleville, Ontario

Library and Archives Canada Cataloguing in Publication
Stiller, Brian C.
        What happens when I die? : a promise of the afterlife / Brian
C. Stiller.
Includes bibliographical references.
ISBN 978-1-894860-43-7

        1. Future life. I. Title.
BT902.S74 2011   236'.2   C2011-906387-5

CASTLE QUAY BOOKS

Dedicated to
my father,
Carl Hilmer Stiller (1910–1971),
who taught his family
that be it in living or dying,
greatness is our calling.

CONTENTS

A WORD
FROM THE AUTHOR

I originally had no plans to take on this subject. It was only in discussion with my friend and editor at HarperCollins, Don Loney, that I was challenged to examine what dying is, not just as it relates to the mode or location of our forever-existence but to what it means to us in our earthly living. At first I was reluctant, assuming there was much already that had been said. But after beginning my research, I came to see that my assumption was wrong, and that I was about to be challenged in a personal way and in my faith.

To examine our future life forced me to first reflect on what it means to awake each day to life, today. After I rise in the morning, I head off to a local gym for a workout. My goal is to keep my body in shape for, as I age, I can feel my bones creak under the strain of just getting started in the morning. But there are other aspects of being human that need to be kept in shape, too. And as I began to write this book, I realized I was trapped and consumed by daily issues and guilty of neglecting why I am here.

I do myself good by finding ways to be reminded that life does not end and that what I do in this life reverberates out through the endless years of life beyond death.

For their help along my journey, I want to especially thank Audrey Dorsch who provided editorial assistance in the shaping of the manuscript, in shaping the content and arranging its flow. Joe Couto was a great help in interviews and research; Dr. John Vissers provided a theological review, for which I am so grateful; and Ruth Whitt assisted greatly in keeping us on schedule and in doing a final review of the manuscript.

Lily, my life companion, as always encouraged me throughout this project. She creates the environment so I can set my mind and heart to the text.

As well, this book came about because of our good friends Herb and Erna Buller who believed this project was worth the research and writing, and through their generosity helped make *What Happens When I Die?* a reality.

In the end, the words are mine, as are any shortcomings. It's not that there is a lack of information provided by the biblical text, but rather in my ability to mine its veins and make it plain. Even so, my hope is that the ideas herein will raise a consciousness that life now being lived is preparation for how we will live out our eternal life. Because for you and me, inevitably and irrevocably, this life will end.

BRIAN C. STILLER
February 2001

One

WHY DO WE DENY DEATH?

And come he slow, or come he fast,
It is but Death who comes at last.

Sir Walter Scott, Marmion

When I was born, so long ago,
Death drew the tap of life and let it flow;
And even since the tap has done its task,
And now there's little but an empty dask.
My dream of life's but drops upon the rim.

Geoffrey Chaucer, The Canterbury Tales

One Sunday morning at our summer cottage I awoke to the quiet cries of our daughter, Muriel. I slipped out of bed and hurried into her bedroom, where I found her huddled over the cage of her hamster, Hammie the Hose-Head.

"Daddy, look." She pointed. There in the cage was her beloved friend in the final shakes of dying. It was awful, not just to her tender heart, but to her father, who usually was less than happy with the parents' inevitable task of helping clean up after their children's pets. Now, seeing my daughter in distress, I was surprised to feel loss as well.

I picked up the cage of the now-dead hamster and carried it outside. I didn't have to tell her that never again would she lovingly hold her prized friend or watch him endlessly run on his wheel. I put the cage at the back of the cottage, found a match box, and told her that after breakfast we'd have a burial.

After a weepy breakfast she lined up her older brother and mother. Armed with a shovel, I walked with them into the woods. There, after the final good-byes, we buried the match box containing the dead hamster.

"Where is the hamster now, Daddy? Is he with God in heaven?" she asked.

Little girls know the heartbreak of saying farewell to a cherished friend.

Inevitably on this human journey I will die. Though I may live without giving it much thought, at some moment and in some place, life as I now know it will end. People will gather around my casket and look at my waxen face or file by a closed casket with my picture (I hope one of my best) perched on the top; they will speak of memories and times together. Whatever form the funeral or memorial will take, the experience of death is my destiny.

Even so, cultures take extraordinary measures to eliminate reminders of our impending death. It's become a taboo in conversation. For years I've been interested in what life will be like after we die, and so, in various settings, especially with someone who is more senior, I'll ask, "How do your thoughts about life after death change as you grow older?" A shocked expression tells me I've moved beyond the bounds of what they consider appropriate conversation.

We use phrases such as "passed away," "slipped across the Jordan" or "crossed the great divide" to avoid more stark terms about the end of life. Or death is described as an enjoyable journey amid shimmering lights, leading to a flower-filled meadow. Such attempts can either foster the impression that there is nothing of substance after death or that life will go on somewhere in the universe.

As baby boomers age, end their careers, see their children grow up and leave the home, what they'll do with retirement begins to matter more than it did earlier in life. So, like others my age, I regularly check my investments, carefully planning for our future, ensuring that Lily and I will have enough money to provide for reasonable comfort in retirement.

Some years ago, in an enormously popular book, *The Wealthy Barber*, David Chilton described a fictitious barber who, early in his working life, set aside a few dollars a month in an investment account. With the help of compounded interest, by the time he was fifty-five years old, the barber was a millionaire, with more than enough to retire on. About the same time an insurance company launched a successful ad campaign on the theme "Freedom 55," based on the premise that if you plan and invest properly, you'll have enough to retire by the time you are fifty-five. You can then kiss your job goodbye and sail off into the blue, spending your life in Florida or Arizona, relaxing on a beach or a golf course.

Yet, while we spend enormous amounts of time researching and planning to make sure that life during retirement will be good, few of us give much thought to what life after death will be like or consider how we can shape that existence. Why is that? Could it be that we assume we have little or no influence over what will come, much as we assume we have little to say about our time of dying? Or could it have more to do with how we divide life: the physical body on one side and the spiritual, or soul component, on the other? In a world shaped by science, the idea of a nonphysical world has been viewed with skepticism and cynicism. Dualism is the result. We've learned to live in two worlds: the world of the material and the world of the spirit, or soul. And by so doing we define life by what we experience here and now, shutting off the possibility of life beyond a materially defined reality—that is, until we watch a casket lowered into the grave. Then we are brought face to face with the question, "Is this life all there is to living?"

Segregating life is something we've learned to do quite well. Those who attend church will be reminded by worship, prayers, Scripture, and sermons that quality of life does not equate with material possessions. But then we travel to work on Monday morning as if what we heard the day before has nothing to do with how we work, or the aims or objectives of our employment. Driven by the bottom line, our lives tend to be founded on the premise that life's achievements are best evaluated by what we own.

The extraordinary rise in the number of services providing financial counseling and investment strategy and management has skyrocketed. The astounding number of people involved in stock-market investment is a powerful signal that our multiple generations are shaped by a conviction that life is dominated by material and physical well-being.

Yet alongside this enormous preoccupation with the "Wealthy Barber" syndrome another movement parallels the baby-boomer drive to financial security, and that is what is sweepingly called "spirituality." Influenced by both New Age and charismatic Christian ideas percolating out of the last part of the twentieth century, books dedicated to the search for life beyond the material, addressing topics such as "conversations with God" and "journeys of the spirit," have jumped to the head of the best-selling book lists. These, along with apocalyptic material, fit with the search for the spiritual. Both rise out of a deeply felt need to connect with life in a way not defined or limited by traditional scientific definitions.

When Princess Diana died, call-in shows were plugged with questions such as, "Where is she now?" Following the deaths of John Kennedy, Jr., and his wife in a plane crash, American talk-show host Larry King invited a priest on his program to answer that question.

When death comes without warning, we search for some

WHY DO WE DENY DEATH?

sort of logic, forced to ask the larger cosmic question, "What is its nature and extent?" In those moments a materialistic definition of life is both cold and inadequate. Driven by fear and loneliness, we search for ultimate values. It is then that the acquisition of things pales in comparison to our need to see life beyond the present and to hope that our loved one has not ceased to exist, but is now in a place and state that are real and substantive.

I came across a web site that speculates on when a person will die.[1] I plugged in my date of birth and was told that my predicted date of death was Saturday, May 21, 2016, which meant that by their calculation I had some 493,527,620 seconds of life left. Though I plan to live longer than that, it is a reminder that death is as sure as tomorrow's sunrise, and that with each passing day my life is shorter.

In Jesus' time the average life span of a Roman was twenty-two years. During the Middle Ages a human's life span rose to thirty-five years. By 1840 in England, it had reached forty-one, and by the time my father was born in 1910, female North Americans lived fifty-five years on average, and males fifty-two. By 1945 that average had risen to sixty-six years. Today in Canada it's 75.7 years for men and 81.4 years for women.

Today, death is covered by our antiseptic world of hospital gowns and paramedics and capped off at the end with kindly funeral directors. We go to extraordinary lengths to beautify the corpse, pay significant sums for funeral services that provide viewing rooms for guests, arrange for flowers, plan the memorial, organize a caterer for food following the service and then, in some cases, sit for a couple of hours listening to accolades and stories and memories. At its heart this elaborate scheme is a desperate need to soften the harshness of death and postpone the inevitable loneliness and sorrow.

But what was it like a hundred years ago, out on the prairie landscape, for my grandparents as they were forced to witness and deal with death? The entire family would be part of a loved one's dying moments. They would hear the last words, the last gasps for breath. They would see the body stop functioning. The cries of pain would cease, the words of goodbye trail away. The body would become stiff, the face lose its color, becoming pale and pasty.

Then family and friends would gather around the corpse— minus embalming fluids and preparation. In those small rural communities a funeral was a rite of passage, as the loss of one person upset the equilibrium. In that era death was "in your face"—not in the comfort of an efficient funeral home with personnel who handled the difficult details. Not in a large cemetery disguised as a park. But right there. In the home. The burial in the cemetery in the center of town, where family members passed every day. Ignoring death then was difficult.

So, while astounding advances are being made for the betterment of human life, we distance ourselves from the actual event of dying, hiding it away from our own living. We keep those who are dying behind the curtains of the intensive-care unit. The aged we move to a nursing home. We feel guilty about moving elderly parents into such facilities, where they will receive the more extensive care they need. But we solace ourselves—and so we should—that they will be better off compared to our attempting to care for them at home, where tension and unrelenting annoyances can make life miserable for everyone.

Regardless of our good reasons for doing what we believe is best, as a culture we shelter ourselves from the death moment. How much easier it is to arrive at the funeral home after the embalming is complete and the dead person is nicely laid out in a coffin. Led by a courteous staff we walk softly into a quiet room where we observe our loved one in silence, or grieve along with friends and family.

On the flip side is the fascination death holds for us. What news bulletins get our attention? Someone famous has died. People will not soon forget what they were doing the day they heard that John F. Kennedy had been shot. For weeks headline writers worked with increasingly bizarre creativity to tell the world the gory and minute details of everything from the grassy knoll to various conspiracies. Newscasters know what pushes up their ratings: killings, accidents, and fires.

And so while we go out of our way to distance ourselves from death, we are still exposed, over a lifetime, to countless numbers of deaths in movies and television. It is estimated that by the time the average North American child graduates from high school, he or she will have watched forty thousand violent deaths. The daily fare of violence pushes death—often horrible death—in our face. Blockbuster movies depict mayhem and violence. Death is all around us, though mostly at arm's length. As much as blood and guts are part of the regular fare for movies and books, we segregate that from real life with the rationale that it's just fiction.

Like most artists who want living, breathing persons to sketch and paint, we want to avoid the lifeless. Not surprisingly, we avoid going into the rooms where medical examiners perform autopsies. But could it be that by such compartmentalization, by keeping the dying out of sight, we lose the benefits of seeing death as an inevitable part of living? Since death is as real as birth, it is my conviction that our lives are enriched as we consider what death means in life, and the impact that life today will have on what happens in the hereafter. For surely the matter of life after death is inevitably linked to what I do in life to prepare for death.

Even so, regardless of how we handle death, when it comes, it seems so unfair. Unless the person who has died has lived to an elderly age or is in such desperate physical stress that dying is a relief, we see death as a thief—as it is. While we may not have thought much about death, when we receive the sudden and shocking news that a friend or family member has died, we have the sense to know that life is more than breathing or the heart beating. Life has a quality compared to nothing else and we measure it by its quality. In our wills my wife, Lily, and I have given instruction that if our lives so deteriorate that we can be kept alive only by machines, the medical authorities are to disconnect them. We know that having to sustain our breathing and keeping our organs functioning by mechanical means is not what we call life. Life implies a quality of living and that sense of "good" living plays itself out in our vision of what life after death will be like.

In this attempt to understand the nature of life after death, we run into a roadblock because of our notion of time. Einstein's theory of relativity postulates that in traveling at the speed of light, time stands still, which leads to the idea that if one goes faster than the speed of light, time reverses. Now try to translate that into living. Life is so earth-centered that to conceive of life beyond our parameters of time befuddles the mind.

In the Western world we view time on a linear paradigm, in which time moves from the past to the future in measurable units. It has a beginning and an ending. Eastern religions see life as cycles, in which life goes from one body to another after death. Regardless of how one sees time—be it linear or cyclical—we act as if life revolves around us. This egocentric view diminishes our understanding of time outside of either time-paradigm, and makes it difficult to imagine what is going on with those who have died, those who now live outside our current time framework.

Our sense of spatial realities also complicates our understanding of an afterlife. Even though our understanding has expanded over the centuries, we are stuck with being able to see only our universe. The ancients viewed a universe in which many gods lived in the heavens, evidenced by the impact the sun, moon, and stars had on the earth. As the moon controlled the tides, and the sun the day, the night, and the seasons, so the ancients believed that it was the many gods who ruled over human life.

In Dante's *Divine Comedy*—one of the most important books on life after death—the fourteenth-century writer builds a seven-tiered heaven and a three-tiered hell, with God living in the highest heaven and Satan in the lowest hell. This view changed during the Enlightenment, as the ideas of heaven and hell were seen as metaphorical rather than physical. Then Isaac Newton changed our view of the relationship of God to creation by describing life as a machine God created, leaving it alone to run on physical principles. His theory was called Deism.

During this period of the Enlightenment, creation was no longer seen as having been designed by a loving and caring God. The instant fame of Darwin and his theories of natural selection heightened the view that life on planet Earth was not the result of a sure-handed designer, but rather the haphazard evolving of a chance development of all species, including humans.

Underlying this was the conviction that science was the only means by which one could discover and determine what is truth. Telescopes and microscopes were but the beginning of a surge of scientific thought that became the prime framework of research. This scientific preoccupation opened the way to understanding human personality and social interaction in the newly designed "sciences" of psychology and sociology. So, for example, Freud interpreted religious beliefs within the ego and id, and sociologist Max Weber attributed the rise of capitalism out of the beliefs and social influences of the Protestant community led by the Reformers, Martin Luther, and John Calvin.

Shaped by two philosophical views—rationalism and empiricism—the increasingly dominating world of science distanced itself from discussion of the supernatural, viewing such matters as only belonging to the world of religion: rationalists seeing truth as the result of thought and empiricists asserting that all that can be known is to be learned only from our senses. Thus science and logic became the accepted foundation by which theories or beliefs would be tested. As a result, propositions not tested in this scientific way would be rejected.

In such a world ruled by science, ideas such as the afterlife, because they were not testable, were deposited in the basket of fables and feelings. Serious work on the afterlife would then be left to the paranormal.

This diminishing of the importance of understanding the afterlife was tragically reinforced by some churches and theologians who interpreted the Scriptures in such a way as to discredit much of what the Bible had to say about life after death, interpreting texts that describe heaven and hell as being so metaphorical as to mean little about what life beyond death might be.

There came a swift reaction against this reduction of the Bible to fables and myths. Resisting the hold of the scientific world, various religious movements jumped beyond the boundaries of reasonable debate and research, including in their repertoire ideas and persons that tended to discredit the search. Religious cults and groups emerged, promoting various visions of the end of time. Some ended up like the Jim Jones mass suicide or the Heaven's Gate cult of southern California.

Even with these bizarre and tragic results, the genie of spirituality has been let out, and the resurgence to find what is beyond life on earth is changing the face of the Western world.

The preoccupation with a materialistic universe wore thin as people saw past such narrow thinking, seeing rather that human life is more than the sum total of its physical parts.

Rejecting the juggernaut of science, beginning in the 1960s, a religious upheaval helped to rewrite our sense of the real, incorporating the spiritual as legitimate. While some of this search for spirituality led, at times, to religious quackery and even though much of what passed for insight was nothing more than verbal mumbo jumbo, the human instinct for the non-material could no longer be rationalized away. Today this search continues with remarkable strength and dynamism.

Two

CAN NEAR-DEATH EXPERIENCES TELL US WHAT LIFE AFTER DEATH IS LIKE?

To die, to sleep—
To sleep—perchance to dream: ay, there's the rub,
For in that sleep of death what dreams may come
When we have shuffled off this mortal coil,
Must give us pause . . .
the dread of something after death,
The undiscovered country, from whose bourn
No traveler returns, puzzles the will,
And makes us rather bear those ills we have
Than fly to others that we know not of?

William Shakespeare, *Hamlet*

On Thanksgiving Day, 1999, London, Ontario, broadcaster and columnist Jim Chapman went to the gym for his usual workout. He felt terrific. For the first time he ran a full mile, then went through the rest of the workout routine his trainer had prescribed. As his head touched the mat after his final ab crunch, Jim knew something was wrong.

Knowing that heart disease ran in his family and having interviewed people about medical issues, Jim had a pretty good idea that he was having some sort of heart incident. He tried to shake it off, in case it was just a muscle strain or something.

It didn't shake off. One of the other fellows in the gym called an ambulance.

"By now I'm starting to realize that not only does this have the possibility to be something serious, this *is* something serious," Jim recalled in a personal interview. Despite the intensity of his situation, Jim remained clearheaded and aware of what was going on. "I remember this very clearly, because right in here somewhere I said to myself, 'You have to pay attention, you have to take in everything that happens to you. . . . You may find a lot of fodder here for a story about the medical system.' "

After his fiftieth birthday, eight months earlier, Jim had endured several months of deep anxiety and was preoccupied with a very real physical fear of dying. Although he didn't articulate it at the time, he felt a "sense of impending doom."

"I tried to physically stave off this melancholy by getting myself into as good a condition as I could so that if the end of my life was really the end of everything, then at least I'd add a few extra years to enjoy whatever was worth enjoying." Now, as he watched the paramedics strap him into position in the ambulance and hook up the IV, Jim remembered thinking the words, *"When does the fear start?"*

"I thought very objectively, 'Well, what do I fear?' Well, I have a terrible pain in my chest—that doesn't feel very good. I'm sweating—that's not very comfortable. But I don't have that feeling in the pit of my stomach—I don't have that fear there."

The ambulance bounced down the road to the hospital. Out of the ambulance and into the emergency room. Still no fear. In fact, he was calm enough to experience a moment of anxiety about his appearance. "Oh, this is great—all these people—and I'm in my gym shorts and a ratty old T-shirt." He thought of all the times he'd seen people being wheeled into hospitals on TV and how often they were panic-stricken.

"I thought, 'Geez, I'm not freaking at all. I'm very calm and cool about this. Ah, this is great. I'm not afraid.'" By this time it was harder to stay totally conscious because he'd been given drugs, but he was still taking it all in—asking the doctor about some of the changes to the provincial health-care funding and whether that had affected his job.

After about twenty minutes in the emergency room he experienced an overwhelming feeling of weariness. He decided he wasn't going to be able to stay tuned in to what was happening. He'd have to close his eyes, just for a minute.

"I closed my eyes and the room fell silent. All the noise disappeared. And I thought—very clearly, because all of this is crystal clear to me—that something must have happened. *Open your eyes and see what happened.* I didn't want to open my eyes. *Open your eyes and see what happened.* I opened my eyes and I wasn't in the ER anymore."

He was standing in a meadow, with a stream running across in front of him from left to right. The meadow overlooked a low valley to a little ridge of hills. Everything was in shades of brown.

"I thought to myself, 'I've died—they lost me.' I was absolutely convinced I was dead. How else do I explain what's happening here? And the way it had happened? It wasn't as though I kind of faded off into some dreams and faded into hallucinations or anything. One instant I was there, wide awake and cogent in the emergency room, and the next instant, in the blink of my eyes, I'm standing in this field. No kind of confused or delusional transition period." Then his family began to materialize, as though they were behind a gossamer curtain. He could see them, but they didn't see him. For the tiniest instant, Jim felt that fear he'd been waiting for, and the fear was that he wasn't going to see them again. But as quickly as it came, it left and he was filled with a communication of some sort.

"I didn't hear it, but it was within me. There was no doubt in my mind that this was a message to me. And the message was, *Don't worry about them. They love each other, and they'll be alright.* . . . As soon as I had absorbed that message—however long it took, which wasn't very long—they faded away."

As his family faded, the presence grew stronger within him.

"It wasn't outside of me; it wasn't somebody else speaking to me; it was within me. And this presence again is communicating to me, but it's not talking to me—it's not words. It's some other kind of communication. But the message is very clear . . . reinforcing . . . that my old life is over, that I'm moving now to something else.

"I was filled from my toes to my nose with a feeling of contentment and peace and tranquillity that those words don't even begin to describe. . . . I knew I was in the presence of God. . . . I didn't know exactly what God was in that context, but I knew that I was in the presence of God . . . in the presence of the creator . . . in the presence of everything. And this feeling continued to grow, and it was the most wondrous experience . . . overwhelming. I could just sit here and give you adjectives all day and I still wouldn't even scratch the surface of how overpowering that feeling was."

Then Jim began to experience a new message; he was being welcomed, being "called home." His thought processes were still very clear.

"I'm still Jim Chapman; I'm still the guy that a couple minutes ago was lying on that table in the ER. Now suddenly I'm in this suspension of reality, but I'm still me. I'm very conscious of being me. But I'm going home, I'm going home, I'm going home."

Then he became aware of the presence of an infinite number

of "souls" or entities. He couldn't see them, but he knew their presence, both as a collective body and as individuals, though he did not recognize anyone, and none communicated directly with him.

"I had an absolute sense that . . . I was going to go and join that whole. I was going to become part of that. I had no sense of, or no concern about, being lost in that enormity of this thing. I had every sense that I would continue to exist. I had every sense that I was going to something that was going to be beyond anything I'd ever experienced, largely because of the peace and the tranquillity I felt, the sense of completion, the sense of being part of this greater thing, yet still being myself— going home."

He was receiving another message that he didn't realize until later: Here's the riddle of the universe and here's the answer. You've been looking for the riddle of the universe; here's the answer, Jim.

After he'd been there for some time, he began to feel a little nonplussed, because he didn't know what to do. There were no signposts, no instructions, nobody walking toward him with an idea. The communication he was receiving was not dealing with his predicament right then.

"Well, light in a tunnel. I've heard a lot about lights in tunnels—better look for the tunnel. . . . I started to look around—there was no tunnel. What in the heck am I supposed to do? I can't stand here forever."

As that thought occurred, his attention was attracted to the low line of hills across the valley. He noticed a couple of bright lights on the hill.

"I thought, 'Well, there's some light. I guess I better walk toward it. That's what you do when you're dead.'

"As I walked across the field toward the light, I was still feeling fabulous but was not receiving any more information.

16

Then I saw a face of an angel, appearing in front of me with no robe or wings, just the face of a young woman.

"I just had time to think, 'What do I do now? Do I say something? Does she say something?' when she yelled at me, 'Mr. Chapman, are you in there? Can you hear me?' I blinked, and I was back in the ER and she was the nurse."

Jim wasn't immediately cognizant of the importance of what had happened to him. He didn't know until later that his heart had stopped for two and a half minutes.

Near-Death Experiences

Jim Chapman, like many others whose similar experiences have been recorded, had what Raymond Moody, in his 1975 bestseller *Life After Life*, called a near-death experience (NDE)—the experience of being clinically dead and then returning to life.

Moody, a professor of philosophy, describes how, in 1969, a student approached him to say, "Dr. Moody, I wish we could talk more about life after death in this philosophy class." Moody was curious as to why the student wanted to discuss a topic he had never considered for philosophy. "Because about a year ago I was in a bad accident, and my doctor said I died. I had an experience that just totally changed my life, and I haven't had anybody to talk about it with."

Moody invited the young man to his office and heard a story that was strangely similar to one he had heard from Dr. George Ritchie, a professor in psychiatry who claimed to have been pronounced dead, and yet who to Moody seemed quite sane. With these two accounts from seemingly reputable persons, Moody set out to research the topic. After interviewing some 150 people that medical staff had ascertained were clinically dead and who then had been resuscitated, Moody wrote his book.[2]

Moody was one of the first researchers, along with Elisabeth

Kübler-Ross, Dr. Kenneth Ring, Dr. Michael Sabom, and Dr. Melvin Morse, to bring the subject of near-death experience to the public in the mid 1970s. A 1994 Gallup Poll estimated that at least 12 million adults in the U.S. alone had had an NDE. In 1996 that figure moved up to 13 million. Sociologist Reginald Bibby estimates that some 1.3 million Canadians report having had a near-death experience. Given the reluctance that many have in speaking about their experience, the numbers could be even higher. Although most people who have come close to death say they remember nothing, a third or more later report that "something happened." That "something" might be a near-death experience.

Moody's book opened the door for further research and writing. People began talking about it with their friends, providing all sorts of descriptive and anecdotal material for talk shows and books. Elisabeth Kübler-Ross, a psychiatrist whose work focused on death and dying, became the most popular of researchers/writers on NDE.

Moody's book, while setting loose a debate over whether such experiences are valid, also defined a typical near-death experience. He wrote:

> A man is dying and, as he reaches the point of greatest physical distress, he hears himself pronounced dead by his doctor. He begins to hear an uncomfortable noise, a loud ringing or buzzing, and at the same time feels himself moving very rapidly through a long dark tunnel. After this, he suddenly finds himself outside of his own physical body, but still in the immediate physical environment, and he sees his own body from a distance, as though he is a spectator. He watches the resuscitation attempt from this unusual vantage point and is in a state of emotional upheaval.
>
> After a while, he collects himself and becomes more

accustomed to his odd condition. He notices that he still has a "body," but one of a very different nature and with very different powers from the physical body he has left behind. Soon other things begin to happen. Others come to meet and to help him. He glimpses the spirits of relatives and friends who have already died, and a loving, warm spirit of a kind he has never encountered before—a being of light—appears before him. This being asks him a question, nonverbally, to make him evaluate his life and helps him along by showing him a panoramic, instantaneous playback of the major events of his life. At some point he finds himself approaching some sort of barrier or border, apparently representing the limit between earthly life and the next life. Yet, he finds that he must go back to earth, that the time for his death has not yet come. At this point he resists, for by now he is taken up with his experiences in the afterlife and does not want to return. He is overwhelmed by intense feelings of joy, love, and peace.

Later he tries to tell others, but he has trouble doing so. In the first place, he can find no human words adequate to describe these unearthly episodes. He also finds that others scoff, so he stops telling other people. Still, the experience affects his life profoundly, especially his views about death and its relationship to life.[3]

Michael Sabom, a cardiologist, describes two phases of near-death experiences, which he calls *autoscopic* and *transcendental*. The autoscopic phase begins when people recognize they are dead and then sense they have left their bodies. Many report watching themselves from the ceiling as medical staff care for them. Most report they have great peace about what they see and are not anxious about what is happening. Free from the pain associated with the attempts to resuscitate, they watch the often-frantic efforts to bring their bodies back to life. Though they are able to observe their anxious loved ones, they aren't able to communicate with them.

The transcendental state follows. The usual report is that the people begin to move through a tunnel. As they do, they see a light at the end. In this phase, many report that they hear forms of music or gentle, reassuring sounds. Some claim that an angel or spirit guides them through this phase. Eventually they emerge from the tunnel and are surrounded by brilliant light. They are then met, often by friends who glow with an inner light and joy. These might be friends or relatives who have died, or even manifestations of Jesus, Buddha, or Allah, depending on the person's faith. Some will be given something of a "tour." Some are given a choice to remain or return to earth, though most are instructed to return to earth because their work on earth is not yet finished.

In his studies, Sabom discovered that only one-fifth of near-death experiences included both the autoscopic (out-of-body, during which the person continues to live) and transcendental (moving into another world, at which time the person is clinically dead) phases. In his studies, one third went through the autoscopic phase and half experienced the transcendental phase.[4]

In *Beyond Death*, Gary Habermas and J. P. Moreland examine near-death experiences in which the subjects describe events and details they had no way of knowing.[5]

- Katie, a young girl, almost drowned. Her brain was badly swollen and she was kept on an artificial lung and given a 10 percent chance of recovery. Three days later she not only described what the doctors had done but told in minute detail what had gone on at her home: details of what her family ate, where they sat and even the toys her brother and sister played with.[6]

• An eleven-year-old boy, after being in cardiac arrest for twenty minutes, had no heartbeat. He later claimed that he watched as doctors and paramedics attended to him from his vantage point on the ceiling. When asked what had happened, he described in accurate detail the procedures, who was there, what each was wearing and even their conversation.

Cardiologist Fred Schoonmaker studied some fifty-five patients who had had near-death experiences while their EEG recordings were flat (indicating no brain activity), some for several hours. One woman with no vital signs and a flat EEG reading, for three and a half hours, lifted the sheet from her face as she was being wheeled to the morgue. After the shocked orderly returned her to the ward, she described in detail what had gone on during the attempt to resuscitate her, even recounting a joke someone had made in an attempt to lift the tension.

Habermas and Moreland tell of a woman who claimed she saw a young man standing alongside an angel. She was surprised to see him and said, "Why Tom, I didn't know you were up here!" He said he had just arrived. After being told she would return to earth, she awoke to find herself on the hospital bed. Later that evening she learned that their friend Tom had died that day in an automobile accident.

Kübler-Ross, after she had interviewed many from around the world, said, "In all the years that I have quietly collected data . . . every single child who mentioned that someone was waiting for them mentioned a person who had actually preceded them in death, even if by only a few moments. And yet none of these children had been informed of recent death of the relatives by us at any time."[7]

Accounts like this seem to be common. Records have been gathered under careful scientific procedures to ensure the highest possible accuracy. Habermas and Moreland describe how the research has been systematized by a number of scientists, adding credibility to the increasing amount of anecdotal material describing the out-of-body and near-death experiences people have.

Patterns of NDEs

No two NDEs are identical, but within a group of experiences a pattern becomes evident. The pattern is that any single experience includes one or more of these elements:

- Feeling that the "self" has left the body and is hovering overhead.
- Being able to describe later who was where and what happened, sometimes in detail.
- Moving through a dark space or tunnel.
- Experiencing intensely powerful emotions, ranging from bliss to terror.
- Encountering a light. It is usually described as golden or white, and as being magnetic and loving; occasionally it is perceived as a reflection of the fires of hell.
- Receiving some variant of the message, "It is not yet your time."
- Meeting others, maybe deceased loved ones, sacred beings, unidentified entities, and/or "beings of light," sometimes symbols from one's own or other religious traditions.
- Seeing and re-experiencing major and trivial events of one's life, sometimes from the perspective of the other people involved, and coming to some conclusion about the adequacy of that life and what changes are needed.

- Having a sense of understanding everything, of knowing how the universe works.
- Reaching a boundary—a cliff, fence, water, some kind of barrier that may not be crossed if one is to return to life.
- Entering a city or library.
- Receiving previously unknown information about one's life, i.e., adoption or hidden parentage, deceased siblings. (Very rare.)
- Deciding to return. This may be voluntary or involuntary. If voluntary, it is usually associated with unfinished responsibilities.
- Returning to the body.

Many people say they have glimpsed the pattern and meaning of life and the universe, or have been given information beyond an ordinary human capacity to gather such knowledge. What is clear is that every type of NDE reveals issues of deep significance to the life of the individual and to humankind in general.

Not all near-death experiences are loving and positive, however. For most people the experience seems to be joyful beyond words, but others tell of unpleasant or terrifying experiences. These may include feelings of panic and anxiety, a sense that they are entering a dark, foreboding world of sin and evil. Some perceive the light they see to be a reflection of the fires of hell. As this is quite rare, most studies ignore its reporting, staying with the positive NDE reports.

One extraordinary aspect of NDEs is that the underlying pattern seems unaffected by a person's culture, belief system, religion, race, education, or any other known variable, although the way in which the NDE is described varies according to the person's background and vocabulary. There is no evidence that the type of experience is related to whether the person is conventionally religious or not, or has lived a "good" or "bad" life according to his/her society's standards (although an NDE often affects how life is lived afterward).

Those who report a near-death experience say it is one of the most powerful experiences a person can have. In many cases it permanently alters a person's perceptions of what is real and important. Pam Barrett, a former politician in Canada, had a violent reaction to a dental anesthetic. While the dentist was working on her teeth, her throat swelled and constricted her breathing.

"It changed me instantly," she said. "I knew I had to start a clean page. That's not easy to do, but it's what I have to do. I have to do some very serious spiritual exploring . . . I made the sign of the cross and died. I was on the other side long enough to feel the peace of God, the lack of questions—there are no questions left—and the incredible relief and comfort. It was a wonderful, warm, gray mist, a soothing environment. I was without challenge or pain and, most important, without fear. When I was dead, all I knew was that this is the ultimate happiness."

Although before her NDE Barrett was a lapsed Roman Catholic, she viewed death as being the end. Later, in her out-of-body experience, she received the indelible message that she must find new paths in her life. It came as a feeling, but she knew the words to put to the feeling. Leaving her political career, Barrett set off in search of that new life.[8]

Barrett's response is not singular. Moody found that those who described such an experience became more altruistic, less materialistic, and more loving. Dr. Bruce Greyson, a psychiatrist at the University of Virginia Medical School who has spent much of his medical life investigating these "peepholes" into life beyond, says that those who claim to have had an NDE "become enamored with the spiritual part of life, and less so with possessions, power and prestige."[9]

But is it real? Medical technology may be able to bring patients back from the edge of death, but science is not able to explain what happens in the process. For people who believe that only physical events can be real, the NDE—or even the idea of such a thing—may be disturbing or seem ludicrous. How can NDEs be explained?

From a medical perspective, NDEs may be simply hallucinations produced by a chemical reaction in the brain. Some hallucinations might be the result of abnormal neuronal activity in the temporal lobe of the brain. Michael Persinger, a neuroscientist at Laurentian University in Sudbury, Canada, says that by stimulating the brain's right temporal lobe (the area responsible for perception) he can induce the sensation of moving through a tunnel of brilliant white light, similar to the reports of many of the NDE claimants.

A problem with this explanation is that those who underwent Persinger's test also experienced "lip smacking, nausea, distorted color perception, hallucinations of geometric patterns, pain, disorientation and so on,"[10], experiences that are quite unlike those reported in NDEs. So it seems that another explanation is needed if near-death experiences are to be seen as invalid.

Studies on NDEs suggest that those who report such experiences show no selective difference based on age, sex, socioeconomic standing, educational level, religion, or attendance at church, synagogue, or mosque. One study did show that those claiming an NDE reported a higher incidence of childhood abuse and a more difficult home life than the average.[11]

To some people, a near-death experience suggests occult activity. It is true that some who have made the near-death experience central to their research and writing have had some occult or spiritualistic involvement. Hillstrom claims that Raymond Moody, Robert Monroe, and Elisabeth Kübler-Ross all have "unusual spiritualistic affiliations."[12] Though this doesn't discount their work, it does place their studies within a larger world of modern New Age-style thinking and experimentation.

Sociologist Allan Kellehear, not surprisingly, sees these experiences through the eyes of his discipline. For him, a person's social experiences play an enormous role in what they see or hear. For example, an Indian living in a world of Hindu images, would see those images in the near-death moment. To Kellehear such experiences are not abnormal but "are surprisingly common, normal responses to uncommon, unusual circumstances."[13]

We may or may not accept such explanations, yet the phenomenon cannot be dismissed even if we cannot explain it. Whatever the near-death experience is, it is neither recent nor local. Experiences have been reported through the centuries, from many cultures and religious traditions. Something happens, and it changes people's lives.

Because of the significant percentage of North Americans who report a near-death experience, there is a growing acceptance that there might be something beyond death, after all. While there is the normal amount of skepticism when a well-known person relates such a story, talk with people in the coffee shop and you'll soon see the nodding of heads when you ask if this stuff can really be believed. Add to that the rise of New Age-style religious interest, and the numbers of those who accept the NDE rises dramatically.

Many people believe that the NDE proves there is life after death in a literal sense. For the more cautious, the experience is not proof, but it suggests that some aspect of human consciousness may be independent of the body and may survive physical death. However, whether one sees the meaning of the NDE as religious or secular, there is much to learn.

My task is not to prove or disprove near-death experiences. However, given the extraordinary nature of such experiences and the accompanying scientific research, we ask whether there is sufficient material from which we can draw conclusions. Are they simply hallucinations or self-delusional episodes?

Sabom, while beginning as a skeptic, concluded that near-death experiences have to be more than just what a person has imagined. In his research he asked those who claimed to have had an NDE to give in detail what they saw during the time medical personnel were trying to resuscitate them. He found a strong correlation between what the person reported and what the medical records showed the medical staff were doing. This isn't proof, but in the early years of research into NDE, at least he showed there is something beyond self-deception.[14]

But what does NDE say about life after death? Even though some people have experiences that seem to take them into another world, does this prove that life exists beyond death? And if it does, does it give us any sense of what that life might be like? Gripping though the NDE stories are, and as life-altering as many seem to be, the big question is, do they provide a substantive enough foundation on which to build a view of life after death? Books describing conversations with God, a vision of heaven, or a new theory on the soul fill our library shelves. For every new era and culture another idea emerges purporting to be the most accurate or revealing about life beyond the physical, and it races to the lead in book sales. With the growing interest in things spiritual, these stories, though compelling, still force us to ask whether they give a glimpse into the future sufficient for us to decide how we will live today.

When one takes distance from the emotional grip of a tear-inducing account, there are concerns about whether these stories can be relied on as indicators of the future. As much as one does not wish to discount the honest intention of the story-giver, they simply do not take us far enough into the afterlife to provide any substantive information.

For example, any identifiable religious figures that appear during an NDE seem to fall in line with the person's experience. In a study by Karlis Osis and Erlendur Haraldsson, Christians report meeting Jesus, Jews encounter angels, and Hindus see Shiva, Rama, or Krishna.[15]

Osis and Haraldsson also report that no Christians or Jews met a Hindu personality and that five times as many Indians met deceased figures as met religious ones. Indians claimed that 23 percent of the figures they met were women; with Americans it was 61 percent. Other researchers noted that Indians were taken to the nether world by messengers; when they arrived they were met by a gatekeeper who, after consulting papers, concluded the messengers had taken the wrong people and therefore sent them back to earth. Such variations make it seem that the nature of the NDE (though not the occurrence of the experience) is culturally influenced, rising out of one's life experience.

Hillstrom notes that many who have had an NDE describe a long tunnel with a light at the end, the beauty and serenity of what they believe is heaven, meeting relatives and friends and seeing religious figures such as Jesus or angels. Most cases suggest that what people encounter is happiness, love, and beauty. Few tell of meeting with unhappiness or a hellish kind of world. However, cardiologist Maurice Rawlings observes that in his research he found as many negative as positive near-death experiences. He suggests that the reason so few are reported is that people are reluctant to talk about them, or they find them so fearful they repress the memory. He tells of a cardiac patient who slipped in and out of consciousness. When conscious he pleaded with Rawlings not to let him go, for he believed he was slipping into hell. Later when asked about it, the patient said he couldn't recollect that experience.[16]

I'm fascinated by the stories of those who have had something within their dying experience, something which obviously was life-changing. I was riveted by Jim Chapman's story. This is what he saw. I'm not going to deny that this was real to him during his two and a half minutes of death. His story, collected among thousands of others, is impressive.

However, as impressive as they are, they give us no clue as to what life after death will be like. To the degree that they collectively affirm that death is not the end, we must turn elsewhere to learn what life beyond death is like.

Three

WHY DO WE FEAR DEATH?

Ay, but to die, and go we know not where;
To lie in cold obstruction and to rot;
This sensible warm motion to become
A kneaded clod; and the delighted spirit
To bathe in fiery floods or to reside
In thrilling region of thick-ribbed ice;
To be imprison'd in the viewless winds,
And blown with restless violence round about
The pendant world; or to be worse than worst
Of those that lawless and incertain thought
Imagine howling: 'tis too horrible!
The weariest and most loathed worldly life
That age, ache, penury, and imprisonment
Can lay on nature, is a paradise
To what we fear of death.

William Shakespeare, *Measure for Measure*

A vital part of thinking about death is to ask, Why do I fear death? Few I've known say they look forward to death. This is understandable. Life is all we know about, and we want to hold on to as many days of living as we can. Survival is deeply imbedded in us. So when my car spins out of control and I face possible death, my life flashes through my mind in miniseconds. In desperation I instinctively cry out, "God, save me." To fear death is not surprising.

The great storyteller Leo Tolstoy walks us through the fear of dying in *The Death of Ivan Ilych*. We see in Ivan what to me is the most frightening reason to fear death: to have lived life and to judge it as having been meaningless. As a member of the Court of Justice, Ivan has been called on to judge others. Now he turns to his life and does the same. His career in the government has been characterized by a series of promotions. Careful to do what was expected of him, he obeyed authorities, for that, at least, was minimum.

Finally a promotion gave him the income to buy the elegant house of his dreams. His preoccupation with decorating the house led him to become involved in the work. While demonstrating how the curtains were to be hung, he fell and struck his head. At the height of his career this accident, which seemed so minor, led to his death. In his last days, confined to bed, he had no choice but to look on his imminent death. As he does, he sees the emptiness of the life he has lived.

In looking back, all he can find of value is his childhood. From there, life—at least as he sees it from his deathbed—went downhill. So now, in his final days, life for him is "senseless and horrible."

"Maybe I did not live as I ought to have done," he wonders. "But how could that be, when I did everything properly?" and he immediately dismissed from his mind this, the solution of all the riddles of life and death, as something quite impossible.[17]

After some time, Ivan finally admits that he has lived a deception. "'Yes, it was all not the right thing,' he said to himself, 'but that's no matter. It can be done. But what is the right thing?' he asked himself, and suddenly grew quiet."[18]

Then he dies. All he has built in life is defeated in death. Observes writer Roy Perrett, "This is why he suffers so much in the face of death, for what he has lived for is rendered meaningless by death."[19]

For Ivan, power and control was the stuff of life which, in dying, he had to let go. But in life it was this obsession with power which kept him oblivious to what he was doing to others. Only in dying does he see the enormous burden he has been to his family. In seeing it, death has forced him to look full in the face of his lifelong failure. In the final moments he gives up control and releases his family from "these sufferings."

I understand Ivan's fear of that which forces us to see who and what we are. The tragedy for Ivan was that he lost his opportunity to learn in life. In denying death we insulate our hearts from learning what death has to teach us. For Ivan the lesson comes too late, "for his death renders meaningless the life he has led by destroying that to which he is so attached: viz. power and control."[20]

Tolstoy forces us to wrestle with Ivan's worthless life without resolving it by adding on eternity. Tolstoy's underlying question is, "If there is no tomorrow, what do I need to do to make life on earth worthwhile?"

That leaves us with these options: if there is nothing after we die, then we must do what we believe is best for this lifetime, for that is all we have; however, if there *is* life after death, then best we try and get a sense of what that may be like. For if what we do in life affects what happens to us later, it is important to shape these "three-score years and ten" to our advantage. But before we examine that, it may be helpful to explore why we fear death.

Robert Neale, in *The Art of Dying*, identifies three reasons for fearing death: fear about what happens after the moment death occurs, fear concerning the actual process of dying, and fear over the loss of this, the only life we've known.[21]

I stood by the bed of my wife's uncle in the hospital in New Westminster, British Columbia. He was in his final days of living. He had lived his life with a strong Christian faith. As we talked I could see fear in his eyes. I asked, "Are you afraid?" He nodded, not speaking, although a tear, followed by another, slipped quietly down his cheeks. For us all, fear of the unknown is as natural as any emotion.

We wonder about and perhaps fear what will become of our bodies. We may visualize our bodies decaying, lying months and years in a rotting casket in a forgotten grave. If we choose cremation, knowing our bodies will end up in ashes can generate feelings of loss.

Many also fear judgment, a basic tenet of the Christian faith. As much as we would like to believe that God is really a nice fellow who'll overlook our peccadilloes, there is anxiety about meeting God. The Christian gospel is framed by the idea of accountability between the creator and created. Thus, in facing death, we are struck with sheer terror at the thought of meeting God, unless we can be sure our failings will be excused.

There is also the fear of not knowing what form future life will take. As firm as one's beliefs may be—even if one sincerely believes there is a life to be lived after death—none of us knows what that life will be like. And that uncertainty can induce fear. A friend had never been in an airplane. She was looking forward to her first flight but was fearful. I asked why: she had seen planes flying; she had watched documentary films about flying and had talked with friends who had flown many times. But she had not done it herself, and until she felt the plane surge forward and lift and eventually touch earth again, she would fear flying. Not unlike dying. Though we have snippets of stories of those who say they have ventured across the divide and returned, and even though we may have a deep-rooted belief in what life will be like, death is an enormous shift of all we've known.

We not only fear what will happen to us after we die, we fear the very process of dying. The very thought of hospital life triggers in me a sense of discomfort. When I think of friends enduring chemotherapy—which brings them to the brink of death, only to be pulled back for a few weeks and then to start the cycle all over again—I can only hope I'm never in that situation.

We also fear being stripped of our dignity. Nothing reduces us all to a level playing field as much as medicine. The Queen endures what I do. Nothing is sacred. Lying in a hospital ward or in a clinical treatment room, we are helplessly vulnerable, and our loved ones, as well as medical personnel, see our frailties exposed in ways we'd never willingly allow in health.

Most of us pride ourselves on our independence, on not becoming a burden to others. But the process of dying reduces or even eliminates that self-sufficiency. In the hospital we depend on everyone, from house cleaner and kitchen staff to nurse and specialist for all our needs. If we are cared for at home, family members must take from us our independence, leaving us with feelings of frustration or guilt for being a burden.

As we fear what happens after death and have anxiety about the process of dying, we also fear the loss of life itself. As a Christian, I have certain views on what happens after I die. But that is not to say that I won't hang on to this life. It isn't that I'm unwilling to give up this life for something better. It's that I have nothing to compare this life to. This is all I've known. Even those who say life has been rather hellish hold on dearly to life.

While assisting at Grace Children's Hospital in Haiti, I went with a staff member, Gerard, to inform a family that their daughter had died of tuberculosis. As this little girl was one of fourteen children, I assumed that the family would take her loss in good course, sorrowful but not devastated, because they had other children to love and enjoy. How wrong I was!

Gerard parked the Jeep and, carefully stepping our way over and around the refuse and raw sewage running down a crevice in the roadway, we found their home in a shanty-town area of Port au Prince. Gerard had warned me of possible anger toward us, but I thought he was overstating what might happen.

When the little girl's mother saw we were there alone, she assumed the worst. Gerard, in their Creole-French dialect, briefly explained that though the hospital staff had done everything they could to save their daughter, she had passed away that morning. In a flash I saw fear mixed with anger and frustration in the mother's eyes and face. Amid the hysterical weeping Gerard motioned to me that it was time for us to leave. As we drove back to the hospital I realized how wrong I had been. It wasn't that thirteen children weren't enough. Rather it was that in such extreme poverty, life was all they had. And every bit of life was to be held on to—for dear life.

We also know that when we die, anything else we could have done in life is gone. The acorn in each of us calls out to be who we could be. At this stage in life, I've carved out who I am. Though I still have worlds to conquer, Lily and I will have no more children. Our major vocational experiences are coming to an end. We'll continue to enlarge our world through reading, travel, work projects, and our grandchildren, but the conclusion of my major contribution to humanity is within striking distance.

Our fears of death come from our own life experience. I recall my parents saying that when Grandpa Stiller died, he was "ready to go." As a child I envisioned Grandpa standing by the coal stove in the front room of the church manse and just at the right moment, as he was about to die, he would strip off his clothes, drop them through the opening in the top of the stove, and take off to heaven. Now, that's being ready!

As I matured, death took on more of the unknown, and unknowns bring fear. So how do I face that, regardless of my age or physical well-being, I'm dying? Do I see it, as did Carl

Jung, as the fulfillment of life's meaning? Or as Jean Paul Sartre suggested, the ultimate absurdity?

Most of us are successful at blocking out our mortality, living instead in the intensity of today's world. Driven to achieve, we have more than enough to keep us from thinking about death. Many of us live at high speed without giving death so much as a thought.

One can be a practicing materialist—which is to believe that at death we are annihilated—making it one's life-defining faith. Much in our world naturally leads us in that direction. The most dominant scientific assumption in the past 150 years has been Darwinian naturalism. Based on the premise that life is made up of chance encounters of cells, naturalism holds that human life has evolved over billions of years—without any outside designer—into what we are today and that death is the natural ending to a life of biological development. If this is correct, then it's not much of a leap of faith to conclude that, as life began by haphazard fate, there is nothing ahead. Life ends when the cells shut down. Nothing further.

In using the term, *practicing materialist*, I use the modifier "practicing" for a reason. Though most North Americans believe in a theistic religion—Christianity, Judaism, or Islam— many live as if materialism were their working philosophy.

Or one can choose to be an hedonist: "Eat, drink, and be merry for tomorrow we die." It is not a trivial philosophy. Many base their lives on this assumption, defining life by pleasure. The film industry, entertainment, sports, jewelry, cosmetics, much of the travel industry, not to mention many of our eating establishments, reflect our cultural demand for that which gives pleasure. Hedonism, by the intensity of seeing life only in the present and defined only by personal enjoyment, obscures reflection on the afterlife; it becomes a way of putting off having to think about death.

Another way of dealing with the fear of death is to use death as an opportunity to reflect on the life one now lives. In considering death we, in effect, permit the projection of our lives so that, in seeing what we have become, this facing of our past can transfer into personal transformation. For dying is really about living. Facing life is the core challenge. From there we move forward in life, taking on the fears and opportunities as they come, making our own choices and being changed.

One need not end life as did Ivan Ilych, by realizing that it's too late. We need not see destroyed in death what we've built up in life. No one need face the curtain of life concluding that their life had no value. To see ahead to death is to allow it to feed back into life today rather than creating a sense of morbidity, knowing that death awaits wakes us up to the importance of living life well.

Four

WHAT DO PEOPLE BELIEVE HAPPENS TO US WHEN WE DIE?

Make no mistake: if He rose at all
It was as his body
If the cells' dissolution did not reverse, the molecules reknit,
the amino acids rekindle,
the Church will fall.

It was not as the flowers,
Each soft spring recurrent;
It was not as His Spirit in the mouths and fuddled eyes of the
eleven apostles;
It was as His flesh: ours.

The same hinged thumbs and toes,
The same valved heart
That—pierced—died, withered, paused, and then regathered
Out of enduring Might
New strength to enclose.

Let us not mock God with metaphor,
Analogy, sidestepping, transcendence,
Making of the event a parable, a sign painted in the faded
Credulity of earlier ages:
Let us walk through the door.

The stone is rolled back, not papier-mâché
not a stone in the quarry
but the vast rock of materiality that in the slow grinding of
time will eclipse for each of us
the wide light of day.

John Updike

Three primary influences have shaped the contemporary views of life after death in the Western world: theism, materialism, and reincarnation. For our purposes, materialism is of little value. If, as it asserts, life is only that which is material, then life is over at death. Thus, materialism has nothing to offer us in a study of the afterlife.

Theism holds that life is under the watchful eye of the Creator God who, in his wisdom, created all of life and in whose caring hands all of life continues and holds together. Beginning with Abraham, the father of the ancient and contemporary Hebrew/Jewish civilizations, the concept of a single, supreme, and personal God was born.

Though the Greeks were not theists, their views on the existence of soul and body were important to the understanding of the human person and thus the continuance of this entity, especially within the Hebrew and (subsequent) Christian worlds.

The early Greeks, however, were not united on the issue of life after death. Some taught that the soul lived forever, and others that death was the end. Homer taught that at death a person's breath, or psyche, left the body and entered the palace of Hades, who was king of the dead. After leaving the body it continued to exist only as a phantom image that could be perceived but not touched.

Early views included no rewards or punishments for good or bad living, but later these ideas began to have their influence and various secret cults offered believers a state of blessedness after death. These notions became increasingly complex, designating eternal punishment for the severe transgressors while just people would gain immortality, and special ones eternal bliss.

But it was Plato who brought something quite different to the discussion and whose views have had an enormous influence on Western thought. Viewing humanity as combining both the mortal and the immortal, he held that death occurred the moment the soul was released from the prison of the body. To Plato the body was nothing but a place of bondage in which the soul was being reformed.

Even though the warrior Romans were tough politicians, when it came to the life-after-death issue they shifted from their toughness to a kind of romantic spirituality. Greatly influenced by the Greeks, they held that at death souls were taken to the river Styx, where they paid a ferryman to take them across. After crossing they entered Tartarus and were examined by three judges. They would be sent to one of two fields ruled by Hades, lord of the dead.

This world of Greek ideas is important to the understanding of life after death because it stimulated debate among the Jewish community, which in turn influenced early Christianity.

The Hebrew World

In contrast to the Greeks, the Hebrew community did not differentiate between what could and what could not be seen. Their world was pragmatic, earthy, and natural. Their God was not like the Greeks' anthropomorphic gods, but "the God of Abraham, Isaac, and Jacob." Their God was one they could speak to and whose life and destiny was tied in with theirs.

Within Judaism there are three main streams: the Orthodox, who hold to the literal interpretation of the Old Testament, including dietary laws; the Reformed, begun in nineteenth-century Germany in an attempt to modernize Judaism by emphasizing moral issues rather than traditional rituals; and Conservative Judaism, which tried to find a middle path between the two.

None of the three streams has much to say about life after death. For the Hebrew community, life from its beginning focused on life here on earth. The Torah—Moses' five books: Genesis, Exodus, Leviticus, Numbers, and Deuteronomy— gave the early Hebrew tribes instruction on how to live their lives, but nothing about what life might be like after death. As Baal Shen Tov wrote, "If I can love God here and now, why do I need to worry about the life of the world-to-come?"[22]

However, there were occasional glimpses into the future. The ancient Job, who even in his faithfulness loses all he has, suggests that death is all there is: "As a cloud vanishes and is gone, so he who goes down to the grave [*Sheol*] does not return" (Job 7:9). Daniel, a Jew exiled in the hated world of the Babylonians, served the pagan king. In his vision of the future he wrote:

> At that time Michael, the great prince who protects your people, will arise. There will be a time of distress such as has not happened from the beginning of nations until then. But at that time your people—everyone whose name is found written in the book—will be delivered.
>
> Multitudes who sleep in the dust of the earth will awake: some to everlasting life, others to shame and everlasting contempt. Those who are wise will shine like the brightness of the heavens, and those who lead many to righteousness, like the stars for ever and ever (Dan. 12:1-3).

Some Jewish scholars, dating this writing to the latest of the biblical books, suggest that during the period of 170 bc to the time of Christ, rabbis engaged in serious dialogue on life after death because of the enormous assault of foreign invaders in the destruction of Jews. Others dispute this dating, offering evidence that Daniel was written much earlier and that the ideas of resurrection were simply part of a growing awareness among the Jewish community about life existing beyond death, and not an attempt to give some sort of meaning beyond death to counteract the senseless destruction of their people.

For the Jewish community today, the Talmud—the literature written by rabbis just before and after Jesus' time—is critical for their understanding of what life will be like after death. This literature, written between 170 bc and 70 ad (the year Jerusalem was destroyed by the Romans), brings together the doctrine of the afterlife, especially as defined by the Pharisees, who were the prime proponents of life beyond the grave. It was the Sadducees who rejected the belief in the resurrection of the body.

In the traditional Hebrew view, God takes the soul at death for a period of time (not more than twelve months) for purification. The soul is then returned by God to the heavenly "treasury" where it awaits the coming of the Messiah to earth. Some time later the graves open and bodies, made perfect, rise. Their souls are returned to the body and the resurrection of the dead is complete. Today one can see many graves on the hillside of the Mount of Olives, on the outskirts of Jerusalem. Because it is believed that the Messiah will first appear at the holy city of David, Jerusalem, Jews want to be buried close by for first chance at resurrection.

Once resurrected, the person then goes before God in judgment. Those judged righteous go into the life of the world to come, and the wicked spend some time in punishment until they are purified and given the opportunity of entering the final world. Those who don't make it this far are doomed to destruction and have no hope of further life. Gentiles are left out of this scenario.

Even with this view of life in the hereafter emerging out of Jewish scholarship, the modern world has made many Jews look at life more within a scientific framework. Thus, there are now Jews who expect that life beyond death is nothing but a metaphysical fancy born out of hardships and suffering, an emotionally satisfying way of giving meaning to human tragedy.

The impact of Hellenism in the Hebrew world compelled Jewish thinkers to debate this subject of life beyond. This is not to say that there was a convergence of Greek and Hebrew thinking. The Greeks were polytheists, believing in the existence of many gods. For the Hebrews, "the Lord God is one." The Greeks, in their many variations, divided body and soul, creating a picture of a person's soul being immortal and the body being simply the prison of the soul. In essence you could conceive of the person apart from the body. That for the Hebrews was inconceivable.

The Hebrew understanding of the indispensable need for the body to define humanity was a primary building block for Christian theology and a Christian understanding of human personality. Hebrew thinking provided not only a concrete view of God but also of the person.

Jesus' announcement that the kingdom of God had arrived triggered Jewish expectations that the Messiah had finally come, the one who would re-establish the rule of David's throne in Jerusalem and kick out the Romans (or Syrians or Chaldeans or Phoenicians), finally liberating them from the constant harassment of their enemies.

However, as much as they looked forward to a Messiah, Jesus' message of the kingdom of God confused them. Over time, his meaning of the kingdom was made clearer and was explored through what now forms a major part of the New Testament. This idea of God's rule, which the Jews thought of as primarily for them in their Palestinian country, expanded beyond the physical world to life beyond death. This revolutionary idea of life after death exploded the message of Jesus beyond the narrow ethnic and geopolitical boundaries of the Hebrew/Palestinian world.

Views of Islam

Islam, like Judaism and Christianity, is monotheistic. That is, it holds to a single, transcendent, eternal God, creator and sustainer of all life. As life continues, the quality of our afterlife is influenced by how we've lived life; one is conditioned by the other. And God, who created all worlds—what we can see and what we can't—is master and ruler over all.

The *Qur'an*, the holy book of the Islamic faith, describes that the soul at death takes on a new kind of body, one created to live within the new realities of the afterlife. In Mohammed's words, "The conditions of the life after death are such that the eye has not seen them nor has the ear heard of them, nor can the mind of man conceive of their true reality."

According to Qur'anic teaching, life on earth is incomplete, lacking fulfillment. Eternal life not only ties up the loose ends of one's earthly life, but ensures we are held accountable for how we've lived our lives on earth. After death, as the soul begins the process of rebirth, it is greatly influenced by what went on in life on earth, where defects or qualities developed make the soul capable of experiencing joy or pain in the new life.

Muhammad Zafrulla Khan describes, for example, that the sun's light is refreshing to healthy eyes but for sore eyes it brings only pain.

The reactions of the soul in the hereafter will be governed by the condition in which it enters upon that life. A diseased soul will react painfully, very painfully, to the conditions of the life after death. It may suffer indescribable tortures, according to the degree to which its faculties have become diseased during its life on earth. A healthy soul will react joyfully to all the conditions of the life to come.[23]

When arriving in heaven, each will be given a book that he or she must read. On the basis of what was done on earth, reward or punishment will be the result.

Every man's works have We fastened to his neck; and on the day of resurrection We shall place before him a book which he will find wide open. It will be said to him: "Read thy book; sufficient is thine own soul this day as a reckoner against thee." He who follows the right way follows it only for the good of his own soul; and he who goes astray, goes astray only to his own loss. No bearer of burden shall bear the burden of another. (17:14–16)

For the sinner, the afterlife is one of suffering as the person continues with his or her diseased soul. "Lo! who so cometh guilty unto his Lord, verily for him is hell. There he will neither die nor live" (20:74).

However, those who have been true followers of Allah in life will live forever in a pure state of health and bliss. "But he who comes to Him as a believer, having acted righteously, for such are the highest ranks: Gardens of Eternity, beneath which streams flow; they will abide therein forever. That is the recompense of those who keep themselves pure" (20:76–77).

For those deemed to have met the conditions of the faithful, life is forever. Even the sinner can eventually find entrance into the goodness of Allah. Pain and punishment are seen to be of value in curing sinners so that after some time, they too can know the good life supplied by Allah.

For both the righteous and sinner, life after death is progressive: sinners are able to move out of their punishment into a state in which they can react with joy to their surroundings; the righteous, in their constant search for the qualities of Allah, will increasingly experience joy in the surroundings of their God.

The Cycle of Reincarnation

Views of reincarnation have migrated from India to the West, merging with late twentieth- and early twenty-first-century spirituality. Given new life and reinterpreted within New Age movements by popularizers such as Shirley MacLaine, the idea that we live out of many past lives gives people a greater sense of eternal meaning. The failure of North American Christianity to explain eternity as a real place created a vacuum, leaving many looking elsewhere than the church to fulfill the heart-driven belief that there must be something beyond death.

The theory behind reincarnation is that life is a process that goes on and on until we have been taught all the lessons we need to learn so that we can reach nirvana, the state in which, finally released from the cycle of birth, we are sufficiently enlightened to be free to be at one with the Universal Mind.

The source of our Western views of reincarnation comes from a doctrine accepted by both Hindus and Buddhists and in line with Greek philosophy, which spoke of metempsychosis or "change of souls." At its core is monism, a view that all is one, that animal, plant, and human life are alike in their oneness, so that life can move from one form to another. For example, one could be an insect, dog, or tree in another life.

The Hindu view of reincarnation has been westernized by restricting the movement of life after death only to another person and not to an animal or vegetative form. This is a significant reworking from the orthodox version. To use Robert Morey's definition of reincarnation as it is today in the West is a view that ". . . all human 'souls' are involved in a cyclic series of rebirths in which the soul is eventually purged of evil by suffering, administered through the Law of Karma."[24]

This movement has had such a profound effect that some twenty-three percent of North Americans believe they have been reborn from a previous life and that death is but a migration to another life.[25]

Shaping millions of people, this vision of life beyond the grave is based on the notion of karma, meaning I get what I deserve. Somewhere in the universe there is a great scoring "machine" that adds up credits and debits of my life. The karma is added up so that my next life is based on what I've done in the past. The credits and debits are based on how I treat others and live my life: I either end up paying for the evil of my former life or benefit from my good deeds.

In examining reincarnation, flaws appear. One day while walking with Dr. Mark Buntain from his hospital in Calcutta, India, to visit a businessman, we passed a woman and her child picking up garbage beside the road. On our way out after our meeting I asked, "How is it that this man can walk by this woman every day without doing something to assist her?"

"You must understand the nature of karma," Buntain replied. "For this man to help her would be interfering with the process of salvation going on in her life. She obviously is working out of the failures of her past life. Only as she is able to improve her credits and debits—karma—can she build for herself a better life in the next life."

Reincarnation as a religious system is built on the assumption that humans can move up the ladder of goodness, and over a period of time goodness will spread out over the human race.

Journalist Tom Harpur suggests three reasons why reincarnation is less than convincing.[26] First, while it provides for limitless opportunities of life in search for release, one is never able to remember the past life and therefore learn the lessons needed to finally get it right. So, if I don't know why I'm being punished, what can I do in this life to undo what obviously has gone wrong in former lives? Is there any expectation that what I do will better me in the next life? This endless cycle of hopeful improvement seems to have no end.

Even more disturbing is that the cycles assume that life is getting better and that the human community is moving upward on the goodness axis of human existence. Now, that's a hard sell. One need just reflect on the past fifty years, since the Second World War, to see that world society is not improving. There are advanced living standards in many areas, but even in my own country of Canada—which the United Nations regards as the most desirable country to live in—the UN reproves us for the living standards of our First Nations' people.

One small African nation, Rwanda, in recent years had 700,000 of its citizens murdered in a few months. Our ecological systems continue to be pillaged in the driving demand for more commodities. AIDS is exploding in Africa, threatening to obliterate an entire generation. The very best of our educated minds bring to our media a steady stream of stories and visuals, often based on the most sordid of human values, impulses and degrading relationships. And what about the amount spent on illicit drugs, crime, gambling, terrorism, and arms?

I'm not saying that life is not good for many, or that our human enterprise is not generating many wonderful advances. It's just that a view that life is moving upward in the karma of its own existence, learning from one age to another, getting better and better, is naive.

Karma as a working principle is a ruthless way to achieve salvation. It is also faceless, without any sense of being. Even if one's current life cycle is one of comparative comfort, there exists the fear that a mistaken choice or a slip in judgment will prevent one from continuing upward in the next cycle of life, instead damning one to crash downward to the next cycle of pain and sorrow.

Further, what is strikingly absent from this religious worldview is the notion of God. If there is no reality beyond our existence to measure our progress, how is one to know the standards or requirements that enable a person to improve one's karma for the next life? It's tragic but true that the prime example of this view of life after death is played out in the Indian caste system, which is a social framework in which people are trapped for life. Though the government has officially terminated it, it continues to trap people who believe that they are in their position for reasons of the past. It is for them to figure out on their own what is good or evil.

My brother David, while working with an international micro-enterprise agency, sat late one evening with a group of taxi drivers in Bali talking about life. One offered to take him for a tourist ride. After looking at the cab's bald tires, David remarked, "I wouldn't dare trust my life with your car riding on those worn-out tires. Aren't you worried about crashing?"

"One life to another, who worries!" the driver replied.

That led to conversations about what happens when we die. Finally David asked the driver, whose faith was Balinese Hinduism, a regional expression of Hinduism, "What are you hoping for in your next life then?"

The driver described the ultimate hope that his next reincarnation would end in his being a prince.

49

"What are your chances that this will happen?"

The driver slowly shook his head. "I only hope so. I can't bear the thought of going through another life like this."

Within the eternal cycles of living/dying/living/dying, one has no idea whether he or she has attained the good required in this life to ensure upward progression. The dreary existence of many finds no assurance of relief in the next life. Just, "I only hope so."

The Promise of the Gospel

In contrast, the beginnings of the Christian story make it clear that life was never created for death. Genesis begins by describing the one who made it all and under whose hand life exists. Thus, even before we learn of the nature of creation, we learn the name of one-always-before: Yahweh-God.

As we read about those first moments we intuit that life as we know it today, flowing out of the physical DNA of early life, is meant for something greater, and certainly longer lasting than the few short years mortals now spend on this cosmic piece of dust in the universe.

From the critical opening chapters that tell the story of human life on this planet, we are given sufficient detail to help us get a picture of the genius of creation alongside the tragic choices humans made, which resulted in death for the planet, vegetation, animals, and humanity. Strangely, tragically, and beyond the scope of twenty-first-century logic, life is affected by this choice. They turned aside—our first parents—by not only ignoring the advice of the creator, but by belligerently defying him. They were warned, make no mistake about it. They had a choice. There was no compelling reason to decide as they did. They knew in no uncertain terms what would be the result. They may not have perfectly understood the idea

WHAT HAPPENS WHEN WE DIE?

of "death," for nothing had ever died, but the warning had been given.

Out of that world-destroying act they were trapped by the Second Law of Thermodynamics—life winds down, eventually disintegrating. In the process of dying they would finally die. It was not part of the original plan and certainly not the intended destiny of this new and unusual in-the-image-of-God one. However by their disobedience, death results.

The broad sweep of history then documents the way Yahweh moves forward with a plan to turn this forever-to-live creature now dying back to the original intent. The story tells us of their inability—no, more extreme than that, their incapacity—to pull themselves up by their bootstraps and break this death grip. After trying and trying, God steps into human history to accept the penalty of accumulated failure. By his taking on that debt, it is canceled by the Father so that human life is given freedom to rise above death and live out its ultimate mandate.

This Son, predicted earlier in the Hebrew Scriptures, comes in the most mediocre of circumstances, conceived in and born of a Jewish teenager, Mary, before she was married and without her having had sex. In this lonely moment Mary, embarrassed by her pregnancy before marriage, nevertheless carries to full term God's Son, creator of the universe, who, by becoming part of the human race, says in unequivocal terms that the body is not in and of itself evil. It is good. His becoming human makes that very clear.

Now, within the borders of this small strip of land hanging on the eastern shore of the Mediterranean, squabbled over by countless nations for thousands of years, Jesus of Nazareth, living only thirty-three years, not only lays down the radical and earth-shattering message of his kingdom, but in dying accepts the debt of human failure and misery. In rising from the dead he gives visible evidence that human debt has been covered. But more than that, he is the prototype of what we now can be after we die.

Death, a thief and robber, is no longer our final destiny. Broken is the pattern accepted by some, cried out against by others and mourned over by all. Amid all sorts of pagan attempts to soften the blow of death and dying, hoping beyond hope that there is something—who knows what?—beyond, there comes from this one who said himself that he was God, not just a promise but hard physical evidence that for us there too will come an actual physical resurrection. In that future moment our bodies will reconstruct and, uniting with our soul/spirit, live on and on and on and on.

Nothing is more critical or central to the Christian vision of life after we die than a real world, lived in by real people. No disembodied spirits floating in some distant metaphysical world or insubstantial void. We are being returned to the great cosmic plan.

The hobbling, harsh, and debilitating world of suffering, avarice, and hopeless cycles of pain and war will be over. And how does one inherit such a misery-free future? Not by working harder. Not by trying to cancel out failures by better deeds. The promise, this offer of life forever-after-I-die is a gift. A gift? Yes. Not what I earn. Not what I am because of what I suffered. Not what I became by giving away. Not what I rose to be or was able to do. There is nothing I can bring to the negotiations. In coming as I am, the life, death, and resurrection of Jesus of Nazareth is all I need for uninhibited entry to life forever.

That in its essence is the promise offered by the Christian faith. We will live forever as God's people.

Five

DOES GOD EXIST?

In the end that Face which is the delight or the terror of
the universe must be turned upon each other either with
one expression or with the other, either conferring glory
inexpressible or inflicting shame that can never be cured or
disguised.

Our longing to be reunited with something in the universe
from which we now feel cut off, to be on the inside of some
door which we have always seen from the outside, is no mere
neurotic fancy, but the truest index of our real situation.

And to be summoned inside would be both glory and honor
beyond all our merits and also the healing of that old ache.

C.S. Lewis, *The Weight of Glory*

In our quest for an answer to what happens when we die, an
important question is "Does God exist?" If God does exist, and
if our search to understand God's intent for his creation leads
us to believe death is not the end of life, then preparing for that
future should overshadow all we do in life.

If one answers, "No, God doesn't exist," then the definition
of life is left up to that person. Since that is not my starting
point, let me begin with the assumption that humans are built
with an instinct to believe there is a moral universe which calls
us to account, constraining our predilection to self-centered
living. Even if we could logically assert the idea of a cosmos
without God and the follow-up conclusion there is no further
life, we would not be able to escape the inclination to believe

WHAT HAPPENS WHEN I DIE?

that life has design and purpose, and the accompanying nagging conviction that life does not end as our bodies are lowered into a grave. It's also interesting to note that more and more North Americans are showing less and less interest in denying God's existence. The focus has changed.

As university students of the 1960s we were caught up in the "God is dead" debate. Nothing was hotter on campus than discussions about whether God existed or, as Nietzsche said, "had died." That question has turned, and now students, assuming that God exists, are showing more interest in spirituality, a hunger I suspect is driven by a search for meaning in a world of banal pop culture, defined by consumerism, hedonism, and a preoccupation with material well-being. There is a revolution of faith sweeping the world. What has brought this about, and what has shifted the focus away from whether God exists to finding God?

During the nineteenth century Christian faith was shocked by claims that science would finally explain how life came about. In the twentieth century science tried and nearly succeeded in replacing faith as the centrally defining way to understand life, be it in the world of biology or psychology. As science asserted its role in Western living, religious conviction and personal faith seemed less important. Though there were some attempts to challenge their authority, in general, Christian churches accommodated their theories of life to fit scientific naturalism.

That is, until it became obvious that this form of science was going beyond describing the means by which life came to be, to identifying what was believed to be behind the means. By discarding the idea of God, science pushed the boundaries beyond what people were prepared to accept. Working from a hypothesis that matter was eternal, science soon ran into a surprising challenge as other scientists, working from Einstein's

54

theories, postulated the scientific theory that matter is finite, with a point of beginning. Called the "Big Bang" theory, it turned some scientists from assuming that life began without God to viewing the biblical account as being not that far off base, after all. British historian Paul Johnson describes the moment he learned of this, and its immediate impact on what he believed about God and creation.

> Some years ago, I remember listening, or half-listening, to a talk on the radio about the Big Bang which set the entire universe in motion. I suddenly sprang into consciousness and exclaimed, "But this is the first chapter of Genesis, told in scientific terminology!"[27]

Science, with all its wonders and transforming inventions and discoveries, showed its vulnerability as the all-knowing idol of our age. As science was ascending as the seeming source for all human truth, we faced a time when human life was barbaric and massively destructive: the twentieth century. Be it the slave camps of the Soviet gulag, the death camps of Nazi Germany, the American bombs on Japanese islands, the killing fields of Cambodia, or the raping and pillaging of our creation, our world society, in its presumptive atheism, was moving toward self-destruction. "If this is what moral anarchy brings," so the reasoning went, "aren't we better off with God than without?" That two of the worst holocausts were instruments in the hands of atheistic powers—Soviet Communism and Hitler's Third Reich—only reinforced the view that a God-acknowledging world was better off than a God-denying world.

Following the Second World War, there was increased interest in matters spiritual, beginning in the radical, anti-establishment 1960s and growing with the explosive rise of the charismatic movements in both Protestant and Catholic communities, the increased influence of Pope John Paul ii and the moving influence of Islam. As a result, arguments for God's non-existence seem increasingly to fall on deaf ears. Even so, belief in the afterlife is predicated on the existence of God. Without God, discussion about the afterlife is a waste of time. So it is important to reflect on why it is logical to believe in God.

Can God's Existence Be Proved?

When I speak of God I speak descriptively of the One who is creator of the universe, is perfectly good (holy) and fair (just), is present everywhere (omnipresent), knows everything (omniscient), is ruler over all of life (omnipotent), never changing (immutable), and timeless (eternal).

In seeking to "prove" that God exists, it soon becomes clear that one can't. What scientific test would we use? We can't find God by using a telescope. A spectroscope won't reveal deity light rays. A microscope won't tell us of his material makeup. He can't be measured, photographed, or weighed. All those instruments we use to "prove" a proposition don't work in the search for God.

So how can we know of God's existence? At best we can use indicators. Theologian Thomas Aquinas (1225–1274) identified "Five Ways," in which belief in God makes sense. Aquinas wrote these as if he were seeing the creator reflected by a mirror. These ideas act as reflectors, giving hints as to why it makes sense to hold to the belief in God's existence.

Argument 1   We live in a world of motion; it had to have been set in motion by some mover, because for every motion there is a cause.

Argument 2   "Why is there something and not nothing?"[28] What exists had to have been caused. Building on the idea of cause and effect, Aquinas concluded that this world didn't come out of nowhere but was caused by God. Since the world is finite (limited) it doesn't exist independently but is caused. So what caused the universe? This question can be taken back one step to who/what caused the universe? But you can't keep asking that question forever. At some point we end up with the first cause.

Argument 3   Aquinas reasoned that we are "contingent beings." By this he means we aren't necessary to this life and, as such, we had to have been caused. For life to have happened by chance—for a one-celled animal to have come into existence by chance—one scientist reasoned, the odds are one in ten to the forty-thousandth power. Shift that argument to a complex human body and the odds simply skyrocket. The very fact that we are here needs an explanation, which, according to Aquinas' argument, is God.

Argument 4   If there is no God, where does truth and goodness come from? How would we imagine these ideas? Laws don't describe what exists but speak of what should exist. That we expect people to treat us fairly presupposes that there is a right way to be treated. Aquinas reasoned that moral laws don't develop in a vacuum but are expressions of God.

Argument 5   Life is too complex and interdependent for it not to have been created by one who had purpose and design in mind. In seeing a complex design we instinctively assume someone designed it. It has been argued that human life is without design and therefore without a designer. This is like arguing that a group of monkeys left alone to play with computers would come up with a Shakespearean play. All expressions of life, as they grow, show that within their internal codes there is a design or purpose that they live out. What is complex required a thinking, designing mind. For Aquinas the designer is no one else but God.

The very experience of holding our newest grandchild, Olivia Catherine Stiller, keeps me from assuming that such a beautiful tiny girl could be "dreamed" up by the unthinking process of biological chance. The perfect little fingers, dainty and without strength are yet complete, just in need of growing. The eyes, though hazy, are perfect, just needing some time for the muscles to develop to provide focus. So where did the DNA, giving direction to each cell, come from? What kind of God did all this? This question matters much, for this is the stuff of our hope.

While these arguments point out the implausibility of the material universe existing independently, they mostly argue for the exterior matters and don't touch on the personal side of being. These ideas are important in assuring us of the logic of believing in God. But as we move on to trusting God for our eternal well-being, we want answers to questions that are embedded in our persons. For, as humans, we are personal. We are self-aware, flooded with dreams and desires, driven to truth, and imbued with a will to make choices about vocation, family, and priorities. We are also moral beings, responsible for what we do. Being is more than the sum total of body parts and functions. There lies within us the capacity for unbelievable good and unbelievable evil.

If I existed in a world that has no compatibility with these inner realities there would be a basic separation between the two: my personal self and my environment. When I get hungry, I expect my world can satisfy that hunger. Sexual desire is met with the capacity to meet those desires. C.S. Lewis, in one of his few sermons, points out the logic of a world consistent with its inhabitants:

> A man's physical hunger does not prove that man will get any bread; he may die of starvation on a raft in the Atlantic. But surely a man's hunger does prove that he comes of a race which repairs its body by eating and inhabits a world where eatable substances exist. In the same way, though I do not believe that my desire for Paradise proves that I shall enjoy it, I think it a pretty good indication that such a thing exists and that some men will. A man may love a woman and not win her; but it would be very odd if the phenomenon called "falling in love" occurred in a sexless world.[29]

There is a connection between me and my world. It responds to the needs of my body. It follows then that needs of my personhood will find connection and meaning in a moral and personal world. If there is no God to speak to us in our existence, we become nothing more than material artifacts with a thirst and hunger for what doesn't exist. And who are we then? People not only miserable and blinded by despair, but having nowhere to turn for an explanation of our life in this universe.

I have come to know love in many ways and from many people. Is that a freak of nature? Is it only a haphazard colliding of chemical particles in my brain?

And what about reason? If reason allows us to create countless stunning inventions, how am I to understand this if there is no linkage of self to the surrounding world? Does reason operate only inside the human body and mind without connection to our environment and wider world?

Humans also have an inner sense of truth that calls out for symmetry, for a linkage of what I know to be true on the inside to be true in the wider world, be it in this life or life beyond. Ingmar Bergman's movie classic, *The Seventh Seal*, depicts this longing:

> KNIGHT: Why can't I kill God within me? Why does he live on in this painful and humiliating way even though I curse Him and want to tear Him out of my heart? Why, in spite of everything, is He a baffling reality that I can't shake off? Do you hear me?
>
> DEATH: Yes, I hear you.
>
> KNIGHT: I want knowledge, not faith . . . I want God to stretch out his hand toward me, reveal Himself, and speak to me.
>
> DEATH: But he remains silent.
>
> KNIGHT: I call out to him in the dark but no one seems to be there.
>
> DEATH: Perhaps no one is there.[30]

At the funeral of Soviet leader Leonid Brezhnev, then–Vice-President George Bush was reportedly moved by what he saw. Just as a soldier was about to close the casket, Brezhnev's widow pushed past him and, in what was seen as a strong gesture of defiance of an atheistic system, made the sign of the cross on her husband's chest. In a nation that systematically and ruthlessly imposed atheism on its people, she looked beyond the violent suppression of faith. She saw beyond the imposed human vision to the One who, in claiming to be God, died and by so doing gave promise for life eternal; that One who she seemed to know had died so that mercy would be ours. She made that last and final statement of her faith and hopes for a husband who, though ruthless and barbaric in his leadership, might find peace in eternity.

Hans Felix Hedderich, a soldier shot down over the Mediterranean during the Second World War, wrote to his former teacher, German theologian and pastor Helmut Thielicke, from his hospital bed. He told the story of a fellow German who fought against the Soviets.

> We discussed how it was that [Soviet soldiers] died so easily and apparently enviably, letting tanks roll over them rather than surrendering, and still throwing grenades even when they were reduced almost to bloody pulp. Is this greatness, is it heroic, is it madness, or what is it? The young soldier, with what I thought to be the sure instinct of youth, explained it as follows. They died so easily because they had nothing to lose—that is all. What do they really lose when they lose themselves? They do not know the Lord who makes them solitary and non-reprehensible, independent selves. They do not know the "infinite value of the human soul" possessed as the soul of a creature and child of God bought with a price. They feel perhaps that they are only units in a great collective. What do they lose, what do they think they lose?[31]

Without God, the Soviet soldiers' only value was within the collective. Since for them God didn't exist, and therefore nothing is beyond death, they end up having no personal value except what they do for the collective in death. The surviving soldiers saw that the heroic acts of selfless death were desperate acts of people whose faith—materialism—provided no sense that as persons they had value and worth in this life or a life to come. Their only worth was in what they could do for the collective. After that, only death.

This is a back-door example of life without God. Without a God who promises life beyond death, dying becomes the heroic act itself. For one who believes in God, death is not the time when the values of life are made grander but a promise that beyond death, there is more.

WHAT HAPPENS WHEN I DIE?

From children to senior citizens there is a recurring search for God. For centuries the philosophers of our world have structured their thinking and writing around this quest. A line of St. Augustine's is often quoted because it strikes a note at the core of our being: "Thou has made us for Thyself, and our hearts are restless until they rest in Thee."[32] The ancient writer of Ecclesiastes—likely the wise King Solomon—wrote, "Meaningless! Meaningless! Utterly meaningless! Everything is meaningless!" (Eccles. 1:2). And why so? He tells us: "What does man gain from all his labor at which he toils under the sun?" (1:3). The entire book is a gloomy representation of life without God. Wisdom, pleasure, work—they all are just more of the same, grinding out day after day without any sense of its meaning, for without God and the overarching vision of life, life is meaningless. For this writer, if life is not a road to God, then it is foolish and without meaning.

Humanity's drive to find and understand God is centered in who we are, made in the image of God. Try as many alternatives as we might, we aren't complete until we link up with our creator. Plato recognized this. In one of his dialogues he compared us to leaky jars, always in need of being refilled. It seems that most of us at some moment in life walk a dark and lonely road, hungering for light and truth that nothing of our culture seems to satisfy. Oxford scholar Alister McGrath tells the story of an American platonic specialist Paul Elmer Moore who, in his struggle to find meaning amid his bleakness and aloneness, searched for God. Moore writes:

> My longing for some audible voice out of the infinite silence rose to a pitch of torture. To be satisfied I must see face to face, I must, as it were, handle and feel—and how should this be. . . .

Dissatisfaction can set us firmly on the road that leads to

the discovery of a personal God—a God with a face, a God we can handle, feel and name.[33]

Life without God, which by its nature asserts that death is the end, robs life of significance. Human life, riddled with over-whelming disaster, acts of cruelty and, for too many, grinding poverty, in the end is without meaning. There is nothing to redeem the suffering, tragedy, and inhumanity.

Any attempt to discover indications of God's existence always fall short of constituting any sort of final proof. They make sense of our need for God, but they in no way provide anything close to proving his existence.

For belief in God does not come by way of proofs. To believe in God comes by faith. These indicators are just that. While they do suggest that to believe in God is consistent with the world and experience, to believe calls on an act of trust and faith.

This takes us full circle back to the question, "Does God exist?" While God's existence does not depend on my belief, my taking hold of his gift of life does. He will continue to exist forever, with or without my faith. What we will see is that the quality of my life continuance does depend on my answer to the question of his existence in that the responsibility of taking hold of the promise of eternal life is mine. If I believe he exists, at least it is a basis on which I can then consider the options offered.

Six

WHAT IS THE MAKEUP OF HUMAN LIFE?

Do not go gentle into that good night . . .
Rage, rage against the dying of the light.

Dylan Thomas

Life is real! Life is earnest!
And the grave is not its goal;
Dust thou art, to dust returnest,
Was not spoken of the soul.

Henry Wadsworth Longfellow

In our search for answers to what life will be like in the after-life, we must first consider the nature of human life, an issue we tend to ignore. We get up in the morning, prepare for the day, and then work through our agenda. When the body hurts, we go to a doctor for analysis and remedy. When mind and emotions are assaulted we seek psychological help. But seldom do we ask "What makes up who I am?" I know I'm physical; my body is obvious. My mind exists, for I think. Emotions reflect how I feel about myself and the world. The brain, I assume, is where I do my thinking. But when my body runs down, dies and decays, what lives on?

We use *soul* to cover a variety of meanings: "One hundred and thirty-five souls perished in the plane crash," "Bless my soul!" "Christ came to save my soul." This casual usage of *soul* in reference to what is at the heart of who we are creates confusion about our makeup.

We often use the term *immortality of the soul* assuming that what will constitute the eternal "me" is the soul. That's easy to do. Ideas are picked up like lint as we brush alongside various views. If we don't think about what we believe, they confuse and misinform us so we end up muddled about what is the biggest question of all: "What about *me* lives on?"

The immortality of the soul has both ancient and modern expressions. Reincarnation holds that the body—which dies—is simply the temporary carrier of the soul. The soul—which is eternal—lives from existence to another existence in various bodies of human, animal, or vegetable life. The soul's next life is determined by what it has done in the past life. The other view of the immortality of the soul is that after we die, the soul lives on forever as a disembodied entity, never to find its way into another body.

Either of these concepts of the immortality of the soul asserts three essential ideas: the soul is the essence of human life; the soul is immortal in that it has existed forever and will continue to live forever; the body is a prison, which in death frees the soul.

Ideas about body, soul, and spirit in Western civilization are highlighted in the works of Plato, written some hundreds of years before Christ; ideas which have had enormous influence on the world before and after the time of Jesus, right up to today. Plato's view of the makeup of human life is similar to that of eastern religions in that the soul is viewed as being eternal, with no beginning and no ending. The body, for Plato and religions steeped in a belief in reincarnation, is a sort of prison from which the soul seeks release.

Jewish and Christian Views

The Hebrew and Christian view of human life rejects the immortality of the soul and instead teaches that the human person is not eternal but begins at conception, newly created and without previous existence. Furthermore, the person is both body and soul, and although the soul temporarily leaves the body at death, soul and body are reunited in a perfect body in the afterlife. Christian faith sees the person as being body and soul. It is the person, not just the soul, that is everlasting (having a beginning but no ending) but only after the resurrection, so that immortality is a gift and not an inherent constituent of the soul. This promise Jesus makes to those who follow him. Karl Barth said that we are "besouled bodies" and "embodied souls."

Why is it so important that we make this distinction? If the soul—or nonmaterial part of the person—is all that lives on, then life after death will be made up of souls (or spirits) without bodies. And what kind of life is that? Jesus said he was making houses for us in heaven. What kind of house does a disembodied spirit need? And what aspiration is there to live an everlasting life that is completely foreign to all we know about God's good creation? In the act of creating the first human, God "breathed into his nostrils the breath of life, and the man became a living being" (Gen. 2:7). "Livingness" is not an idea in which the body and soul can be disengaged as if one has fullness of life without the other.

The life God created on this planet, in its original intent, had no end in sight. Death came about as the result of human rebellion. The role of Jesus of Nazareth was to restore life. The promise that life will continue in a fully restored form in the afterlife is to return human creation to what it was in the very beginning—a full synthesis of body and soul.

There is another importance to this distinction. By making the body the prison of the soul, the body ends up becoming a necessary evil and not that which, as the Hebrew text tells us, God saw as "good." The image of God is imprinted on human life. In that sense, humanity mirrors its creator and the body is essential to that mirroring. We don't know how, because God is not contained by a physical space, but in reflecting the creator, human creation cannot be stripped of the physical and at the same time be that reflection. The physical creation is as essential to the nature of this part of God's creation as is the soul. To deny physicality as fundamental to our restored eternal reality is simply to miss the point of creation altogether.

The Hebrew Bible does not divide the person and refer to the soul as the essence, but rather sees the person as a unit. It refers to the spirit (*ruah*) as meaning wind, breath, or moving air, which came to mean someone empowered by God. Heart (*leb*), while specifically referring to what beats within the rib cage, became a metaphor for the mental and spiritual center of our being. The Hebrew word from which we get the English translation 'soul' comes from *nephesh*, which is translated as *psychē* in Greek. The word *nephesh* means the person, that is, the whole person.

All three elements in the Old Testament are intermeshed: *nephesh*, *ruah*, and *leb* link together in the wholeness of our essence, the person. So when man was created, God breathed into him the breath of life and Adam "became a living being," or *nephesh* (Gen. 2:7). In the discussion between God and Satan about God's faithful servant Job, Satan is given access to try Job but he must spare Job his life, or *nephesh* (Job 2:6). Psalm 103:1—"Praise the Lord, O my soul; all my inmost being, praise his holy name"—if translated literally would read, "Praise the Lord, O my life, all my inmost being, praise his holy name." Soul and life are seen as the same.

It's true that Jewish theology had little to say about the afterlife. Between the end of the record of Old Testament period and the time of Jesus, the Greek world of ideas, carried on the back of Roman conquest, pushed rabbis to think through what their faith taught about life after the grave. Out of that debate emerged two opposing views: the community of the Pharisees believed there is a resurrection of the body; the Sadducees didn't, contending that life ends at death. It was left up to the newly formed Christian church to further the debate and expand it within New Testament writings.

The early Christians had four Greek words they used. *Pneuma* and *psyche* can be translated as either "spirit" or "soul." *Soma* refers to the body, which includes the body, soul, or the entire self. *Sarx* translates as "unanimated flesh."

The Greek word for immortality (*athanais*, meaning literally "deathlessness") is used only a few times. For example, Paul talks of God "who alone is immortal" (1 Tim. 6:16) and also uses the word in reference to the nature of the resurrected body, which is not corrupted. "For the perishable must clothe itself with the imperishable, and the mortal with immortality" (1 Cor. 15:53). In this latter case, the emphasis is on the resurrected body, which becomes everlasting, meaning that it will then never die.

There has been a debate for centuries over whether the human being is made up of two parts (body and soul) or three parts (body, soul, and spirit). Some scholars differentiate by suggesting that *spirit* refers to the God-image in us and *soul* speaks of our feelings, emotions, and motivations. Most scholars conclude there are just two primary ingredients to human life, body and soul. Throughout the two testaments the two words—*soul* and *spirit*—are used interchangeably, meaning the same.[34] For example, Mary, the soon-to-be mother of Jesus, said, "My soul magnifies the Lord and my spirit rejoices in God my Savior" (Luke 1:46-47 RSV). In the life of Jesus they are used as if they mean the very same thing. In one place, Jesus said, "Now is my soul troubled" (John 12:27 RSV) and in the next chapter, John says Jesus "was troubled in spirit" (John 13:21 RSV).[35]

In two texts, people who have died are called either "spirits" (Heb. 12:23 RSV) or "souls" (Rev. 6:9 RSV). The Bible also refers to people who "have come . . . to the spirits of righteous men made perfect" (Heb. 12:23) and to "the souls of those who had been slain because of the word of God and the testimony they had maintained" (Rev. 6:9). Nowhere does it say that "a soul and spirit" went to heaven. Rather, either *soul* or *spirit* is used. It's as if it didn't matter which word was used to describe the nonmaterial part of human life in its eternal mode.

In death, both testaments use the two words interchangeably. When Jacob's wife Rachel died, "her soul was departing" (Gen. 35:18 RSV). Isaiah, in describing the suffering Savior, said the Lord would "pour out his soul to death" (Isa. 53:12 RSV). In the last moments on the cross Jesus called out in a loud voice, "Father, into your hands I commit my spirit" (Luke 23:46 RSV). In speaking of the nonmaterial part of human life, Jesus identifies the soul as that which continues: "Do not be afraid of those who kill the body but cannot kill the soul. Rather, be afraid of the One who can destroy both soul and body in hell" (Matt. 10:28).

It seems sufficiently clear that both soul and spirit make up the same element of human life and the person is the interrelationship of soul and body.

"The Flesh"

Throughout church history the body is often spoken of as "the flesh," or the fallen side of human life, that which gets us into trouble and keeps us from knowing God. But any view that deprecates the body or flesh does not find its basis in a biblical understanding of creation. When some try to determine the body as the source of sin they fail to note that at creation there was nothing wrong with this flesh.

The Bible does not teach that "the flesh," or physical matter of human life is, in and of itself, sinful or inherently inclined to sin. It does become an instrument of sin and, as such, participates in the rebellion of the entire person against God. Though the body—or flesh—is weak and finite, these terms also describe the soul or spirit. In an ethical sense there is nothing wrong with the body, or flesh. Instead it was the "inner" stuff of the man and woman—what we often call the heart—that was the source of willful disobedience.

The Genesis account tells us that flesh is the physical construct of the man. A rib is taken from the man and woman is made, becoming "flesh of my flesh" (Gen. 2:23). In marriage and sexual union they become "one flesh," speaking not only about their physical oneness in sexual union but about two people joining in relationship. *Flesh* then speaks not only of the body and sexual desire but also of the person.

A songwriter shows how the body and soul together aspire for God: "O God, you are my God, earnestly I seek you; my soul thirsts for you, my body longs for you" (Ps. 63:1). The entire being of the writer is lovesick for God. The flesh is part of that which feels and longs for a relationship with the creator. "My heart and my flesh cry out for the living God" (Ps. 84:2).

In the New Testament, John shocked those who assumed that the physical body or flesh is the evil side of human life when he wrote, "The Word [Jesus] became flesh and made his dwelling among us" (John 1:14).

In speaking to the Hebrew scholar and rabbi Nicodemus, Jesus said, "flesh gives birth to flesh, but the Spirit gives birth to spirit" (John 3:6). Jesus isn't saying that the body is the opposite of the Spirit of God, but all that is human in its fallenness is in opposition to God. As in other New Testament passages, *flesh* becomes a synonym for human life lived in rebellion to God. Paul, in describing the work of God in our lives, said that

WHAT IS THE MAKEUP OF HUMAN LIFE?

our literal, physical bodies had now become "temples" of God (1 Cor. 3:16). If the body is evil, how could God dwell in it? Scripture writers do not see the body as the evil side of life. The body can be used for either good or evil. Even though the body participated in the sinful act of rebellion, it did so no more than did the "heart" or will.

What Is Immortal?

Surprisingly, nowhere in the New Testament is the term *immortality of the soul* used. The word *immortal* is used only in connection with the resurrected body.

> I declare to you, brothers, that flesh and blood cannot inherit the kingdom of God, nor does the perishable inherit the imperishable. Listen, I tell you a mystery: We will not all sleep, but we will all be changed—in a flash, in the twinkling of an eye, at the last trumpet. For the trumpet will sound, the dead will be raised imperishable, and we will be changed. For the perishable must clothe itself with the imperishable, and the mortal with immortality.
>
> When the perishable has been clothed with the imperishable, and the mortal with immortality, then the saying that is written will come true: "Death has been swallowed up in victory" (1 Cor. 15:50-54).

Note that "the perishable" or "the mortal," which refer to the human body, will be clothed with "the imperishable" or "immortality." Paul is specifically saying that the body will become immortal. This stunning announcement shuts down any notion that the body is evil with no eternal value in God's economy, or that our afterlife is lived without the body.

The human being is a psycho/pneuma–somatic (soul/spirit-body) unity. A friend once said, "I wouldn't recognize a soul if I tripped over one, but I'd sure see a person!" How close he was to understanding the nature of human life, both here on earth and in the afterlife. In some religious circles we speak carelessly about the soul, as if it is a detached entity of the person. If we'd use the term as the Hebrew and New Testaments do, we would mean the person. For, in our human construct, there is no such thing as one who "has a soul" or who "has a body." Instead, we are a body, we are a soul, we are a being. Together they make up the indivisible reality we call human life.

We bring that understanding into our search for what we'll be in the afterlife. Our life forever is real, substantial, made up of all we are today. Draw a line out from who you are today—dispense with sickness, fears, and proclivity to self-centered-ness—and what do you see? A person fully embodying body and soul, operating in a universe in which there is creative activity and emotional wholeness, a place where you can live at full capacity without the dysfunctions and limitations you know and experience today.

With that understanding of the relationship of the soul/spirit and body, we look at the nature of human existence in relation to its creator.

At the heart of the argument for the resurrection of the whole person is an understanding of our relationship to our creator. This is vital, for it helps us grasp what God is doing in solving the human dilemma and what life will be like after we die.

The *Imago Dei*

To Jews and Christians, being human has a special meaning. Above the surrounding terrain—the multilevels of vegetable and animal life—human life is unique, without parallel in the universe. We have this remarkable phrase: *imago Dei*. That is, "created in the divine image." This resemblance to God characterizes humanity, even with its accompanying evil side. As much as darkness tries to snuff out the light of the divine it can't. Woven into the nature of this specially crafted creature are elements that lift us above our neighboring environment. Imbued with what we understand to be essential to the creator God, humanity began life with both intellect and free will. *Imago Dei* is not to be like little gods but rather to have the imprint of the divine. Over the years, within the debates of church leaders, Christian scholars have seen that our life as humans—and I refer to the time before rebellious behavior brought human life into its own demise—began with a status above all other creation.

The Hebrew text puts it this way:

Then God said, "Let us make man in our image, in our likeness, and let them rule over the fish of the sea and the birds of the air, over the livestock, over all the earth, and over all the creatures that move along the ground."

So God created man in his own image, in the image of God he created him; male and female he created them.

God blessed them and said to them, "Be fruitful and increase in number; fill the earth and subdue it. Rule over the fish of the sea and the birds of the air and over every living creature that moves on the ground" (Gen. 1:26-28).

This rich text sets up an understanding of the special relationship between human life and its creator. First we understand that the *imago Dei* means that this special creation is separate from others. As important as the rest of creation is, only humans have this imprint. Along with that is the special role humans are given. They are assigned the responsibility of looking after creation. "The LORD God took the man and put him in the Garden of Eden to work it and take care of it" (Gen. 2:15). In the second account of creation (Gen. 2:16-17) there is another aspect to the *imago Dei*, which is that humans are not only given the task of creation stewardship but are held accountable for how it is done.

Within this calling is something that decidedly does set the human creation apart from the rest, and that is the prerogative given by the creator to the human/created beings to say "yes" or "no" to the creator's stated instructions, provisions, or safeguards.

This carrying of the *imago Dei* goes beyond being a representative, but means we carry within us something that is "like" the creator. This royal "stuff" isn't just about what we are called to do, it has to do with what we are. It's not just talk about a job we've been commissioned to carry out, but about the nature of our bloodline if you like. It is also about our relationship to God. We are truly in the image of God when we stand in right relationship to him.

There is also within the Hebrew world, in its formation under Moses and today, a sense that our identity as the *imago Dei* is not just as individuals but as people in community. Notice the words, *Let us make man in our image, in our likeness.* The *us* and *our*—which find an expression within the Christian understanding of the three persons of God: Father, Son, and Holy Spirit—in this text tell us something about what the one speaking has in mind for the creation. As the creator is "us" and "our" so then are those who are called to be partners, in that the *imago Dei* finds its imprint as well on the community. They reflect as a mirror not just the work but the nature of creator, albeit within the human limitations of the finite world.

The account of Adam and Eve's first child furthers this idea of "being in the image of." "When God created man, he made him in the likeness of God. He created them male and female and blessed them. And when they were created, he called them 'man'" (Gen. 5:1–2). Then it goes on, "When Adam had lived 130 years, he had a son in his own likeness, in his own image; and he named him Seth" (5:3). As Seth reflected the essence of his father Adam, so Adam reflected the essence of his Father, the creator God.

At the time of Noah, with instructions on severe penalties for murder, God's word is, "Whoever sheds the blood of man, by man shall his blood be shed; for in the image of God has God made man" (Gen. 9:6).

Throughout the New Testament there is a running consciousness of this *imago Dei*. The Apostle Paul translates this sense of bearing God's image into ethical concerns about the behavior: "Do not lie to each other, since you have taken off your old self with its practices and have put on the new self, which is being renewed in knowledge in the image of its Creator" (Col. 3:9-10).

There is also a looking forward to that final moment of history when the uninhibited creature will more fully reflect the nature of the image we possess. John puts it this way: "Dear friends, now we are children of God, and what we will be has not yet been made known. But we know that when he appears, we shall be like him, for we shall see him as he is" (1 John 3:2).

To be "like" God takes us beyond our functional calling to our calling to be the creator's presence within the creation. It also speaks of destiny. It points forward to what we are becoming. Not God, for we continue in our finiteness, but a fully actualized completion of the divine design.[36]

In our Western world we have been numbed to this drama by the notion that death is a simple means of liberating our true selves from the restrictions of the body. The coming of

Jesus to earth was to overcome the drastic result of human rebellion. To see this more dramatically, consider the contrast of the deaths of Jesus and Socrates. In this we see the powerful distinction between Greek and Christian thinking on the immortality of the soul and resurrection.

Contrasting the Deaths of Jesus and Socrates

Swiss theologian Oscar Cullmann leads us into this remarkable contrast.[37] It was the Greek philosopher Plato who described the death of Socrates in which death was seen as a relief from the body. As "only an outer garment . . . [it] . . . prevents our soul from moving freely and from living in conformity to its proper eternal essence" (p. 19). So the soul, confined by its outer garment, the body, is imprisoned and death becomes the liberator. "It looses the chains, since it leads the soul out of the prison of the body and back to its eternal home" (p. 20).

Socrates, who looked forward to the poison of hemlock, was not just one who believed in the immortality of the soul, but lived it out in his dying, going to death with composure and peace. "The death of Socrates is a beautiful death. Nothing is seen here of death's terror. Socrates cannot fear death, since indeed it sets us free from the body . . . Death is the soul's great friend" (p. 21).

What a contrast to the death of Jesus. Walking at night into the Garden of Gethsemane, Jesus faces the death he knows lies ahead of him. Mark tells us that Jesus was "deeply distressed and troubled" (Mark 14:33). The looming death pushes Jesus to tell his friends about it. There is real fear, not of the process of dying but of death itself.

He was really afraid. Here is nothing of the composure of Socrates, who met death peacefully as a friend. Now, when death stands before him, Jesus cries to God, whose omnipotence he knows: "Everything is possible for you. Take this cup from me" (Mark 14:36). And when he concludes, "Yet not what I will, but what you will," this does not mean that at the last he, like Socrates, regards death as the friend, the liberator. No. He means only this: If this greatest of all terrors—death—must befall me according to your will, then I submit to this horror. Jesus knows that because death is the enemy of God, to die means to be utterly forsaken.[38]

See the striking contrast. On the day Socrates dies, he lounges with his friends, calmly discussing his death. Jesus, in deep agony of soul, cries out to his disciples to watch and pray. He goes off alone and, sweating what look like drops of blood, goes through the pangs of impending death. As Socrates quietly contemplated death, Jesus wept and cried.

The actual death scenes paint the contrast in even brighter colors. Socrates calmly takes the potion of death and drinks it as if it were the finest vintage in the land. Jesus is given wine to ease the pain and then cries out, "My God, my God, why have you forsaken me?" (Mark 15:34). "This isn't 'death as a friend.' This is death in all its frightful horror."[39] Why the difference? Why could Socrates die with such peace and Jesus with such anguish of heart? For Jesus, this is what he most feared: God-forsakenness, the real curse of death.

Socrates, believing the body was the prison of the soul, actually believed that he was entering into uninhibited freedom. With the chains of the body—the bad self—broken, the immortal soul—the real self—carries on forever.

Jesus, on the other hand, is called to conquer death. "He cannot obtain this victory by simply living on as an immortal soul, thus fundamentally not dying. He can conquer death only by actually dying, by betaking himself to the sphere of death, the destroyer of life, to the sphere of 'nothingness', of abandonment by God."[40] To rescue life, Jesus "calls back the whole man," all that God had created and death had annihilated. Jesus taught the very opposite of the "immortality of the soul" (meaning that life has always been and carries on forever in some form of non-bodily existence). Jesus understood that the body, which along with the soul/spirit is part of God's "good" creation, is destroyed by death. Jesus faced that destruction.

Soul is more than the sum total of mind, emotion, and will. It is that which signals that we are more than material, linking us as partners with God, who is at work in history as the Spirit that does not leave me at death. As the body decays, the soul continues to live on as the eternal Spirit ensures that those who are in Christ have continuity during this gap of time between death and resurrection.

Seven

WHAT CAN WE KNOW ABOUT HEAVEN?

> To enter heaven is to become more human than you ever succeeded in being in earth; to enter hell is to be banished from humanity. What is cast (or casts itself) into hell is not man: it is 'remains'. To be a complete man means to have the passions obedient to the will and the will offered to God: to *have been* a man—to be an ex-man or 'damned ghost'—would presumably mean to consist of a will utterly centered in its self and passions utterly uncontrolled by the will.
>
> C. S. Lewis, *The Problem of Pain*

Golden images of heaven are shaped by childhood stories, nursed along by pictures of billowy figures resting gently, equipped with bird-like wings and child-like faces in sweet rapture seemingly induced by a heavenly Valium: gentle and quiet.

As an active boy, I frankly had no interest in that prospect. I couldn't imagine much worse punishment than to be doped into inactivity. Neither did the idea of sitting around a throne worshipping God day and night (I later learned there was to be no night) sound like much fun. I had a hard enough time sitting through a Sunday church service, let alone thinking it would be heaven to do that forever. In our church we sang a hymn that referred to "that city built four-square." For some time I thought we were singing, "in that city built for squares."

We all grow up with images of heaven, what life might be like after death. But most of us simply strike off such thoughts

79

from our daily agenda and focus on "what really matters," like getting the garbage out or returning yesterday's phone calls.

Our daily preoccupations can change in an instant: a phone call tells of a friend or family member, in good health, now dead from a ruptured aneurysm or car accident. Even when an elderly member of our family dies, we see life in a different perspective and wonder what it's like to die.

At the funeral service we hear Bible readings that hold promise and hope. Hymns comfort us, and prayer seems to place our departed friend within a whisper. Death has a way of making us ask, "What is heaven really like?"

An obvious problem in developing a clear picture of the afterlife is that we work within an earth-bound, three-dimensional, time-contained, space-limited framework. It's in this world that we try to describe what a selfishness-free, love-driven, environmentally-clean, immoral-absent life is like. No wonder we resort to metaphors, images, pictures, and stories to think about life beyond death.

Using figurative techniques is not to say that what is described isn't real. It is a matter of using language as a go-between. We draw on what we know and have experienced as a point of reference to speak about the unknown.

Not surprisingly, biblical writers dipped into the language of their day. When King David said the rivers clapped their hands with joy, he wasn't describing water applauding. Although Jesus spoke of himself as a shepherd, we don't picture him as a New Zealand sheep herder, rounding us up with a Border collie. These are word pictures infused with ideas and filled with breadth and depth of meaning. Jesus, resisting the rabbinical inclination of his day to speak in complicated language, drew on common ideas, objects, and experiences of everyday living to get across his teachings. He was so popular with the people that "the large crowd listened to him with delight" (Mark 12:37).

We post-moderns, living in the twenty-first century, have been fed a steady diet of scientific theories, experiments, and results. We have been taught that the scientific method is the only litmus test. Working within a framework of something being either true or false, we may end up thinking that because heaven can't be scientifically proved as fact, it cannot exist. An experiment cannot reproduce and authenticate the existence of heaven.

There is a concern among some Christians when they hear someone say that parts of the Bible are allegorical. This concern is understandable given the slippery slope of twentieth-century theology, in which the Bible was sometimes read so much in terms of metaphor that events such as the resurrection of Jesus were interpreted as not being literal but as speaking only about the idea of new life.

It needs to be understood that to use literary devices isn't to say the subject being described is not actual, substantial, and true. Take the description of heaven, for example. The Scripture says its streets are paved with gold. Whether gold is the literal paving substance is not the point. The view of heaven draws on what we see as having enormous economic value. We say in effect, "Heaven is so incredible that what we consider to be rare and of great value here will be in plenty there, and what we give little value to here will be of enormous value there." In short, it will be a world upside down. To describe the promised city is to try to tell a three-dimensional person what living in a four-dimensional world is like. To convey the eternal to us who are time-bound calls for imaginative language.

A few years ago I coauthored *Lifegifts* with my brother Calvin, a world-renowned medical scientist and a pioneer in organ transplants. Our challenge was to describe to lay people how the immune system of the body rejected an organ transplant and how medical scientists solved this dilemma.

81

One night while we were working on the book, Cal came up with a brilliant suggestion: why not use the idea of an army as a metaphor to describe the roles of the various cells activated by the immune system in protecting the body from outside invasion? So he named the various cells by army titles. The metaphor made clear the roles of various cells in protecting the body.

Communication by metaphor is going from what we know to what we don't know. To help us understand the kingdom of God, Jesus used parables such as "A farmer went out to sow his seed" (Matt. 13:3). We don't get bogged down in figuring out each part of the story. While the principle of the story is true, the elements of the story provide a fictional picture; they become an analogy of what Jesus means. For example, the seed is an analogy for the Word of God; the soil is an analogy for the kind of hearts the Word falls into. God as a poet, musician, historian, and scientist uses whatever is needed to get us from where we are to where he wants us to be.

Jeffrey Burton Russell says it well:

The epistemology [way of learning truth] of traditional Judaism and Christianity opens up toward truth with metaphors that continually grow. Thus heaven is best understood by metaphor. And not only is language about heaven metaphor: heaven is itself the metaphor of metaphors, for a metaphor opens to more and more meaning, and heaven is an unbordered meadow of meaning. Heaven is where language collapses into perfect language and then further—into the truth beyond language. Heaven is what things really mean; it is where all the blurring and sliding amongst terms and concepts and word is caught, finally by i am who i am (God's own name for himself as given to Moses: Ex. 3:14). Human language is baffled by eternity, which is beyond human imagination and reason, except in metaphor.[41]

82

When we talk about heaven we wonder whether it is real. While thinking about how I could make it plain, I prayed, "Lord, help me to see heaven, not just a quick glimpse as some people claim, but something so real that I can describe it as I write." No such luck! Even if I had a dream or a near-death experience, what language would I use? Jim Chapman told me there were no words he could find to describe what he had experienced. In the end, we look to see what writers in the Bible used—pictures, points of reference, objects, common experiences—in our attempt to bridge the wide chasm of understanding. Eternity is real. It's just that our language fails us in the telling.

As a word, *heaven* is often used in antiquity and in current conversation to mean a variety of things. In the Old Testament it was referred to as sky or air (Gen. 1:8), the habitation of God (Ps. 14:2) and angels (Gen. 28:12), and at times it became a substitute word for God (Dan. 4:23).

In the Gospels Jesus speaks of it in several ways: like the Old Testament it is the sky, domain of the birds (Matt. 6:26) and the theater of coming events (Mark 13:25, 26). It is also used as an alternate for God. In the story of the prodigal son, the son confesses that he had sinned against "heaven" (Luke 15:18, 21). As well, it is used to mean the place of future life for those to whom God gives everlasting life (1 Peter 1:4).

Building Blocks to Understanding Heaven

As we proceed, it's important that I give you my underlying assumptions which influence how I arrive at my conclusions about heaven. The way I see the afterlife is shaped by what we know about God and creation. We don't just jump in and speculate on what will go on there without first identifying the nature of God, what he has told us about life, and our makeup as humans. This way of seeing heaven is shaped by nine primary assumptions.

1. *The cosmos is a place of life.* The cosmos, of which planet Earth is but a small speck, was not built with death in mind. We know from the Genesis record and from recent scientific exploration that at some definite time, matter came out of non-matter and Earth was born. On that planet God created life. Life in its origin did not have death as part of its makeup. What the creator began had in it every indication of perpetuity. The creation of Earth and the larger cosmos was for life ongoing.

2. *Human life carries the divine imprint.* Closely linked to that is the creation of Homo sapiens, imprinted with God's image: the *imago Dei*. God said, "Let's make man in our image." The human species was unique, not as a tree or toad, but in its likeness to the creator.

3. *Human nature is life perpetuation.* Like its environment, human life was not designed to die. From its beginning there was no sense that death was part of its horizon. That's where we get this assumption that life continues forever. Humans were not asked to care for the world with a view that existence would end. The hint of mortality was in the promise that disobedience would result in death. But that was a consequence, not a built-in ingredient of the nature of the human creation.

4. *Creation is a physical place.* This creation was not a mirage or place of disembodied spirits. It was real, tangible, and physical. This is so obvious you may wonder why it even needs to be stated. For this reason: to see what life will be in God's ongoing creation, we need to go back to the time when the creation of this planet and humans was completed. The physical creation and the humans, God

called "good." It was as God wanted. There is no sense it was some sort of experiment. What he did the first time was according to his standards.

5. *Work is a gift.* Human life on this planet is to be lived with responsibility. The original creation wasn't a place where one could slack off and loll around on the beach while food magically dropped in one's basket. There was work to be done. It was a place of exertion, responsibility, and progress. God as creator is always creating, and those in his image have that as part of their makeup. The human person continues today to live out of that genetic impulse to create, shape, improve, and grow. Human life has never been about receiving and not giving, being without doing. We exhaust ourselves in overdoing sometimes, but doing is part of our motivation, a part of that God imprint.

6. *Our stewardship is a partnership.* We don't just work. Our working is a partnership with our creator. We join as co-workers in stewardship of the earth. Human life was made to serve this environment entrusted to us so that the creator's expression and handiwork would continue to flower in productive and beautiful ways. This partnership is remarkable. Not only are we expressions of the creator, but we enjoy a working partnership in running an incredible part of the cosmos. This principle of human life, though disjoined through disobedience, never ceased functioning. Today, as abusive as we are of this planet, earth management is still our calling.

7. *Human rebellion brought about devastating results.* Human rebellion broke up the plan. Why God would give humans this option is an important issue, but for another place of discussion. We do know that our first parents were aware that disobedience would bring death. To what extent they understood what "death" meant, we

don't know. However, sin brought an end to this idyllic world. The impact was so remarkable that it broke the harmony of creation and humanity, pitting one against the other. Today we peer back to see what it was like, but, living on this side of that cataclysmic break, it's hard to grasp its enormity. Humans entered a different phase when they disobeyed, losing their purity and intimacy with the Divine. What was natural became an embarrassment: "Then the eyes of both of them were opened, and they realized they were naked; so they sewed fig leaves together and made coverings for themselves" (Gen. 3:7). They not only hid from each other but tried to hide from God. The resulting impact was global.

The principle is this: the good creation had been shaken loose from it original design and character. The nature of creation as an expression of God had been set on its ear, upset, and changed. This came by way of human defiance.

8. *Death is an anomaly.* Humans, by their failure to live up to their calling, not only brought enormous devastation on the immediate world but imposed onto the genetic moral and physical structure of life a morbidity, that is, an inclination to dying. In scientific terms it's called the Second Law of Thermodynamics. This simply states that whatever is, runs down and decomposes. A tree, once it is grown, falls prey to this law and eventually dies and decomposes. With the rebellion of our first parents, this law came into effect, not only for the surrounding physical world of plants and animals but for the human world as well.

The creator had a warning: if you disobey, you will die. And they did. Death was introduced into the scenario of living. Death was not part of the creation design. It is out of the ordinary, breaking the intent of the continuity expressed in the beginning. "God saw all that he had made, and it was very good" (Gen. 1:31). And what he had made did not include dying. It comes as a thief and robber. Death is a disruption, breaking the continuance God had clearly set as human inheritance. Surely not part of the intent of the creator, but there it is. Now, what do we make of it?

As much as we try and make out that death can be beautiful, as comforting as we find the stories of near-death experience, death in the story of human creation is never nice. For it's not only the moment of dying that makes up death; it is the human lot that once we are born we are in the process of dying. Death resides in the very inevitability of it all—not just the event but growing older, losing faculties: Alzheimer's sets in, internal organs suffer disease, the eyes grow dim. In life we are always dying. And that was not part of the design. Death defrauds us of being fully the *imago Dei*.

An episode of *M.A.S.H.* helps make the point. Hawkeye, in trying to resuscitate a dying soldier by pounding on his chest and massaging his heart, yells, "Don't let the bastard win!" Someone asks Colonel Potter what Hawkeye meant by that statement. Potter says Hawkeye was talking about death. When it comes to death, Hawkeye is a sore loser. The image of death as a "bastard" is appropriate: the illegitimate child of the universe in a world gone awry.

9. *Life is restored by the resurrection.* The final principle underlying my way of seeing heaven has to do with the nature of Jesus' body in the resurrection being the prototype of human resurrection. We know now the nature of our body's afterlife. It is not, as the Greeks claimed, a disembodied spirit, floating in an ethereal heaven. Neither is it

the transference to another incarnation or life. It is rather the substantial, physical reality we know as the human body. This remarkable pattern promises us that the afterlife is one in which we will live, in many ways as we do now, in our physical bodies restored and free of sickness.

These nine assumptions are the way I see the future. The physical creation was made to last without ending. Human life, imprinted by its creator, was given the implicit promise of everlasting life and all of this was within a physical world. Human life as part of that world worked—growing, developing, thinking of new ways of tending the creation. We not only worked, but as stewards we were called to "mind the store" of God's creation. That came to an end when rebellion broke the relationship. Out of that the thief called death robbed humans of the promise of ongoing life. But that is restored by the resurrection of Jesus, who provides a real, historical example of the kind of life we will live in heaven.

Out of these nine assumptions I see and interpret what the Bible specifically says about heaven. These are the lenses through which I discern the biblical promises and from that peer into the beyond. So, in understanding that, how are we helped in seeing the life beyond? This way: by seeing what God prepared in the beginning we can better see what heaven will be like, for by his own action—through his son Jesus coming to earth, dying, rising from the dead with a resurrected body, and the promise of a newly created world—he ensures that his good creation will continue as it was. The problem having been fixed, what he began will now continue.

Drawing on Eden, heaven becomes clearer. In the first garden, where human life began to live out its calling as God's image, life was as good as one can imagine—and better. Heaven will not be something out "yonder" but on earth. Renewed and perfect. As human life was called on to care for (be stewards) and give oversight to the physical world, so we too will live in a world that is physical, real, and productive.

As I write, I look out over Beaver Lake, a beautiful haven teeming with life, growth, and beauty, but also decaying—a world where animal life and vegetation is born, lives and dies all within the life cycle of the world as we know it. So what will be different about heaven? It will be a physical world but with a difference: missing the cyclical pattern of death and dying. As much as I try to imagine such a world, I can't. However, by reading the pages describing creation, I know it will be substantive. Will it be Beaver Lake? I'm aware of the danger of trivializing heaven, as if it will be not much more than earth is today.

The other danger, which we've been drawn to throughout most of the Christian era, is to play with metaphor to the extreme. In so doing, we mystify heaven so much that we strip it of its physical reality, viewing it as a place and time of "harp playing" with expectations bordering on the bizarre, not unlike the magic world of Disney or Harry Potter. We must not get locked into pictures which deny the reality of the afterlife. Heaven will not be a world of quasi-fairies and see-through floating beings. We must not be trapped into turning the resurrected Jesus—who in very real terms describes what we will be and the nature of our new bodies—into something other.

What I'm driving at is this: heaven will be a place consistent with what we know creation to be. Here are some of our common questions about heaven.

Will We Be Human as We Are Now?

The answer to this requires that we draw not so much on metaphor as on history. The body of Jesus following his resurrection is a clear statement of what our bodies will be like in heaven.

His resurrected body was physical: he ingested food and was seen by human eyes. It had nothing of the mystical characteristics that often shape our views of what our bodies will be like in heaven. For example, some believe that Jesus passed through solid doors or walls in meeting with the disciples. But the text doesn't say that. It just says, "When the disciples were together, with the doors locked for fear of the Jews, Jesus came and stood among them" (John 20:19). The locked doors tell us that the disciples were terrified, which was the point Luke was making. Jesus may very well have knocked on the door, telling them who was there and they would have opened the door as later happened with Peter (Acts 12:12-17). However, in our retelling, we've given Jesus—without any biblical support—a body with ability to pass through walls. Now, it may be that he could do that, but this text doesn't say so.

The Apostle Paul puts it this way in speaking of the kind of body we'll have: "The body that is sown is perishable, it is raised imperishable; it is sown in dishonor, it is raised in glory; it is sown in weakness, it is raised in power; it is sown a natural body, it is raised a spiritual body" (1 Cor. 15:42-44).

Being imperishable, the body won't grow old, weak, or wear out. Gone will be disfigurement, abnormality, dysfunction, and disease. Paul's reference to "dishonor" relates to the body's various problems, whether from birth, accident, or disease; there will no longer be anything "dishonorable" or unattractive about our bodies. The word *glory*, used frequently throughout Scripture, suggests a radiance that will, in a sense, show off who we are.

We also will be "raised in power." This suggests something beyond being free from disease, injury, or disability, but rather, possessing a remarkable strength. This is not to suggest some "God status," but a power that matches the original creation.

When Paul speaks of a "spiritual body" (*pneumatikos*) he

doesn't mean nonphysical, but the physical body at the level of perfection consistent with the first creation and the resurrected Christ. Paul's contrast of the "natural body" with the "spiritual body" is not to distinguish between the physical with the nonphysical but to say that the natural person is subject to the demands and desires of this age, governed by a human will out of sync with God. His promise is that our natural person will be raised into a perfect person in the new creation.[42]

Paul makes two other references to our resurrected bodies. "He who raised Christ from the dead will also give life to your mortal bodies through his Spirit, who lives in you" (Rom. 8:11) and "[Jesus] will transform our lowly bodies so that they will be like his glorious body" (Phil. 3:21).

After resurrection, our bodies will have similar form to that which they had in life, yet perfect in strength, youth, and glory. There was a fascinating subplot at the time of Jesus' resurrection. Matthew tells us that many "holy people" who had died and come back to life somehow worked their way out of the tombs and appeared to people in Jerusalem. Now, apart from scaring the daylights out of their friends, that they were recognized suggests that the resurrected body is sufficiently like our earthly body to be recognized.

A common objection to the idea of physical resurrection is the question of how a body that has been cremated, eaten, and digested by animals, decomposed in the sea or vaporized by an atomic blast can be reconstructed into a physical being. Here, as in other cases, it's important that we don't decide it's impossible simply because we don't understand the process by which it will be done. God both continues to create us and to create us anew—*ex nihilo*—"out of nothing."

The Apostle Paul never says that the old body will be raised. Several times he uses phrases such as resurrection *of the dead* (I Cor. 15:12) and *from the dead* (Phil. 3:11). By using these phrases he is saying, in effect, resurrection is not of the old corpse but of the dead person. "He has in mind the emergence of deceased persons from the real—of the dead in a transformed bodily state."[43]

This promise builds on the premise that God created human life so that both creator and created would live in this cosmos in engaging and satisfying relationships. When this relationship was disjoined by human mutiny, God had a plan by which the consequence of death would be overturned and the creator and created would reunite. For that to happen, the dying human needed a means by which a perfect body and soul would be reconstructed. Jesus provided that in his resurrection and promised the same for us. How will it come about? I don't know. That God stands behind the promise is sufficient.

Heaven will not be a place in which we move about as disembodied spirits. Even as I know the substance of my body as I write, in that place and time of heaven, I will be physical, substantial, and real. My friends will look at me, know who I am, and I'll continue as the person I am, with identity, personality, and will.

What Will We Know?

Our person—the perfect and full integration of the body and soul—will not be divine. As much as Adam and Eve were the *imago Dei*, living in a perfect world, they had limitations. They didn't know all things; that is, they weren't omniscient. Their knowledge, understanding, and physical abilities had boundaries. Just because we will be in the unhindered presence of God doesn't mean we will finally have all our questions answered.

I sometimes hear people say, "When I get to heaven I'm going to finally learn why my son died young." Maybe not.

We will still be living within the limitations of being created. Closely though our lives will mesh with the creator, God will remain all-knowing, but we won't be. As well, the questions that posit themselves so unremittingly on our minds today may not even matter then.

Will There Be Sex and/or Procreation?

Jesus, in responding to a Sadducee's question about whose wife a woman would be in heaven, said, "When the dead rise, they will neither marry nor be given in marriage; they will be like the angels in heaven" (Mark 12:25). Nowhere else do we hear anything more, but it seems procreativity will no longer be necessary. As well, given the absence of moral fallenness, our relationships will be different. The unique oneness of Adam and Eve as part of their perfect world speaks about relationship that is powerful and all satisfying. Although sexual intercourse was provided for procreation, it went much further, symbolizing the oneness of the two persons. However this subject gets no further treatment by any New Testament writer which leaves us no more informed than to say we don't know.

What Will Be the Dimensions of Heaven?

Looking up at a starlit evening sky invites the question, where is heaven? We know that Jesus' physical body left the earth and that he was going to a place; whether that place is within our limited knowledge of the universe we don't know. But where Jesus went is a separate matter from where we will live after death. (For the issue of where we will reside between our death and resurrection, see Chapter 8.)

The place we will live forever is very clear: on God's created planets. The promise about the future is that all creation will be renewed. Isaiah wrote, "Behold, I will create new heavens and a new earth. The former things will not be remembered, nor will they come to mind" (Isa. 65:17). This forms the basis of what John says later, describing his vision of the future order: "Then I saw a new heaven and a new earth, for the first heaven and the first earth had passed away, and there was no longer any sea" (Rev. 21:1).

This new creation speaks of the renewal of the cosmos. Exactly what will be renewed is unclear. Or perhaps it means that the creation is not yet completed. What it does let us know is that at some point God will act clearly and unequivocally to bring all of creation to conform to his eternal design. Peter, in speaking about the last days, writes, "By the same word the present heavens and earth are reserved for fire, being kept for the day of judgment and destruction of ungodly men" (2 Peter 3:7). The new creation will be a continuation of this creation but in a renewed state. Peter's point isn't that the creation will be destroyed, but that fire will deal with the matter of ungodliness. This renewal and cleansing will liberate the creation from its current decomposition.

He draws a parallel with the time of Noah, in which the covering of the earth was submerged by water. The deluge didn't destroy creation but gave it a new start, overcoming the unimaginable evil dominating the world. So whether it will be the continuation of earth but in a renewed state or an entirely new creation we don't know. But it will be a liberated creation from its current decay:

The creation itself will be liberated from its bondage to decay and brought into the glorious freedom of the children of God. We know that the whole creation has been groaning as in the pains of childbirth right up to the present time (Rom. 8:21-22).

This renewing is like the promise of physical resurrection. The creation that in the beginning was good and has since been subjected to the "genes" of evil is renewed so that the intent of the creator is fulfilled. It is into this "new earth" that our lives will emerge and we will take up residence with God: "Now the dwelling of God is with men and he will live with them" (Rev. 21:3).

Our future in heaven suggests an actual location and place. And that place includes planet Earth. Although this environment has been polluted and raped by greed, irresponsibility, and senseless destruction, it will go through a makeover. What God lost in that willful end run our first parents made around God's expressed constraint—and the concomitant results— God's plan is to restore what was lost.

Will We Be Confined to this Planet?

Our ideas of heaven have been so over-layered with images of it being a world of disembodied spirits that it's difficult to think about residing on a planet much as we know now. Yet to imagine the location of heaven requires that we ask again about the nature of God. One thing we do observe is that he is creative. Even within the limited knowledge we have of the universe, it continues to expand. If that is so now, there is no reason to conclude that creating worlds will not go on in the afterlife. Now view this relatively tiny part of the universe within this wider framework of God's creation where creative activity continues unabated. I wonder, what will the creative juices of scientists—then unhindered and working together in complement rather than in competition—produce? Living

WHAT HAPPENS WHEN I DIE?

in that expanding world, will we have access to God's wider world? Given that we have been called stewards, it isn't much of a leap to consider that in heaven we will be given roles beyond this planet.

What Will I Be Like in Heaven?

Heaven will be substantially different from this world in that what keeps life from being good here will there be removed and banished. The rebellious spirit that has typified human life since its early days will be changed. Evil will be extracted and the networks of the kingdom of evil broken. The architect of human suffering and evil will be destroyed, forever banished from human eternal existence.

"The creation itself will be liberated from its bondage to decay" (Rom. 8:21). Human ingenuity will no longer need to focus on ways of preventing disease, pollution, or decay. Imagine what might go on in a world in which all dysfunction and debilitating human conflict is wiped away and we are free to operate in freedom and love in God's renewed world. "No eye has seen, no ear has heard, no mind has conceived what God has prepared for those who love him" (1 Cor. 2:9).

The heart and soul of our place of promise is one in which God—who we now see at best as through opaque glass—will be known and experienced in new and wonderful ways. Again we fall back on the metaphors of beauty, happiness, and unbelievable peace as we try to get a glimpse of that world.

A Bible seer saw ahead and exclaimed, "And I heard a loud voice from the throne saying, 'Now the dwelling of God is with men, and he will live with them'" (Rev. 21:3). The collective wisdom of the ages, all the attempts to figure out the nature of God, the countless books written to describe, exegete, deny, reconfigure the nature of God, will wrap up in our life with God. The life we now know by the Spirit residing in us is but a sample of what we will know there.

Our struggle to find fulfillment and meaning in accomplishments, relationships, and ideas will dissolve. Our desperate struggle to carve out for ourselves a place in the universe will be over. The inner compulsion to write our names on the history of significance will be more than neutralized, it will be absolved. Our lives, driven by competition, will find gentle rest in knowing we are beloved children of the God who began and sustains all of life. Our efforts to figure out why God allows suffering, how it is that some seem favored, and why communities and countries are polarized and antagonized will find their ultimate answers not in the scientific methods of this generation but in the relationship we will enjoy without end.

It's not that we will become God. God is eternal and forever outside of his creation. But there is a sense in which the broken relationship of rebellion is healed and we will walk with him "in the garden in the cool of the day" (Gen. 3:8). Obviously before the insubordination of human life disrupted creation, there was an intimacy between creator and created that facilitated the interflow of ideas. The renewal of creation to its mandate will restore that intimacy.

As this new relationship bonds creator and created, the created will know a heightened level of relationship among themselves. The brokenness of relationship characterizes our fallen world. The beauty of marriage, so perfectly designed, falls into vitriolic abuse when the relationship breaks. The marvel of family is ripped by insensitivity and neglect, renouncing its very intent. Life in the workplace is disjointed by petty self-interests and misunderstandings. Churches too often are torn apart by disagreements that flow more from insecurity and accompanying self-righteousness than from high and lofty ideals.

It is to these human realities that heaven speaks. Being reconciled with God facilitates a love and concern for others that will unburden us from paltry concerns. We will see in each other the goodness and life that will blossom into that which will honor all of life and serve God.

The current ecological disaster is awakening us to what happens when we violate our stewardship of the earth. We have stripped the splendor of wilderness and the bounty of seas by our greed and lack of proper stewardship. We fail to understand that this creation is our responsibility; it is not in servanthood to us. To be a steward calls for serving, not being served. The Hebrew prophet saw it coming: "Because of this the land mourns, and all who live in it waste away; the beasts of the field and the birds of the air and the fish of the sea are dying" (Hos. 4:3).

Now, almost too late, we see the folly of our ways. However, in that future place of peace and harmony this discord between humanity and the surrounding world will come to an end. The principle of survival of the fittest will operate no more. The pervading presence of God will bring relationships of all kinds into mutual support.

What Is the Place of Praise?

One of the central visions John in The Revelation had was people encircling a throne, united in praise to the God of creation.

> Then I looked and heard the voice of many angels, number-ing thousands upon thousands, and ten thousand times ten thousand. They encircled the throne and the living crea-tures and the elders. In a loud voice they sang: "Worthy is the Lamb, who was slain, to receive power and wealth and wisdom and strength and honor and glory and praise!" Then

I heard every creature in heaven and on earth and under the earth and on the sea, and all that is in them, singing: "To him who sits on the throne and to the Lamb be praise and honor and glory and power, for ever and ever!" (Rev. 5:11-13).

This scene lacked appeal for me. I couldn't imagine what God looked like, sitting on a throne. Added to that was the boredom of standing around and singing for eternity. But I've come to see the power of this image for it gives us the sense of participating in an event of enormous proportions. Some years ago I stood with a large international gathering in Lausanne, Switzerland. After joining in an observance of the Lord's Supper we began to sing. The effect was something beyond what I had ever known. It was more than volume; it was a coming together in oneness of spirit. I build on this memory, envisioning tens of thousands in worship. I see the absolute wonder of heaven's collective experience of praise. Seeing the coming together of humanity made free by the Christ who came in death and resurrected power is more than just compelling.

Will I Work?

The image of worship doesn't constitute the whole of our occupation in heaven. Like worship, work in its beginning was a wonderful gift: "The LORD God took the man and put him in the Garden of Eden to work it and take care of it" (Gen. 2:15). Work was an exciting and life-fulfilling opportunity of serving the creator and living in harmony with creation. Work wasn't a result of human disobedience. The instruction to work came before that.

It was only after our human parents broke the creator's instructions that work changed from the harmony of humans and creation to an antagonistic relationship. God spoke in clear terms, describing the changed world in which their call to work would be carried out. The creation underwent a reversal—from harmony of the environment and human life to disharmony. The curse this human defiance brought on all of life was cataclysmic. Adam and Eve heard these words:

> Cursed is the ground because of you; through painful toil you will eat of it all the days of your life. It will produce thorns and thistles for you, and you will eat the plants of the field. By the sweat of your brow you will eat your food until you return to the ground, since from it you were taken (Gen. 3:17-18).

Heaven is when God reverses these world-changing consequences so that men and women will live in a world in which the gift of work is the expression of a loving creator. In looking forward to the new creation we see work, not as defined by life in a fallen world as it was at the time when creation was "good" and work was a joy. That's the framework for heaven.

I have friends who can hardly wait for retirement, counting the months until they live as they choose and not as demanded by the employer. Throughout history, and for many today, work is drudgery, nothing but backbreaking sweat of daily toil. Lacking benefits, medical insurance, or savings for retirement, they live out a work life of demeaning physical tasks. But heaven will change that.

Work of any kind—fishing, building skyscrapers, running a day care, teaching, or writing software—is sacred. Not only were we created for doing good by our work, but we are also expressions of God, who also works: "By the seventh day God had finished the work he had been doing" (Gen. 2:2). Work is intrinsic not only to the created but the creator as well. That means we are in very good company.

But what might our work look like? I'm often asked, "How can I discover God's will for my life?" My first response is to ask the person what he or she would like to do. This often comes as a surprise: "What does what I like to do have to do with what God wants me to do?" This question is based on the assumption that God's will for us is separate from what we enjoy, as if what he has in mind for us might be unpleasant.

God's will falls naturally within my own gifting, so I suggest they begin with these assumptions:

- I do best what I enjoy doing.
- What I do best indicates my gifting.
- God has given me these gifts out of my genetic inheritance, home and social environment, education and experience.
- What God has given to me in gifting he wants me to use in the best way I can.

I apply the same principles to God's intent for us in heaven. But what kind of work will that be? Here we need to allow the underlying principles of God's original masterpiece to come into play, see the world as it was in its unfettered state: a real, physical world where humans and animals were sustained. Unite that world with the very best we know today, and what might that new world look like? Here we are left to our imaginations.

Imagine a workplace absent of selfish reactions, of thievery and of competition over who will get promotion. If our place of employment was filled with deep love and respect for each other, overlaid with a desire to promote the well-being of others, what would that do to the work environment and ultimately our productivity?

The Hebrew prophet looked to the day in which the Messiah will reign:

They will build houses and dwell in them; they will plant vineyards and eat their fruit. No longer will they build houses and others live in them, or plant and others eat. For as the days of a tree, so will be the days of my people; my chosen ones will long enjoy the works of their hands (Isa. 65:21–22).

What Will Be Allowed in Heaven?

Important to the nature of human life is freedom, which opens the question, "in heaven will we be free to choose to sin?"

In the first creation, human life existed alongside the evil force led by Satan. Satan, a senior angel, had led the rebellion against God and by so doing brought evil into creation. It was conflict between Satan and God that led to the attack against Adam and Eve and resulted in their eventual rebellion. The promise is that in heaven Satan and evil will be eliminated from the creation, which in turn leaves no option for the human will to rebel.

But does such a world offer true freedom? This question is seen only within a bipolar perspective of a world in which goodness and evil coexist. In the new world, where God and goodness reign, the polarity is removed, leaving us with absolute freedom to do good.

Unhindered by the boundaries God established for our first parents to protect them from their rebellious nature, in heaven we'll not be driven to test boundaries. People, no longer tempted and tested by the anti-God Satan, will live in a world without evil; they will be driven by the desire to do good and lovingly live in harmony with God and all his creation. It's difficult for us to get our minds around a world in which only goodness is the driving force of human personality. Such is our limited human perspective. God promises that his world of everlasting life is an environment of unbounded life, a new world filled with love and infused with a desire to serve God within an unfettered arena of creativity and exploration.

As stewards of creation, able to move into the wider fields of the universe, it makes sense that we will be able to move about and learn through interplanetary activity. Again, by the very nature of human cooperation, there will be a building together in unity, exploring God's creation as he allows. This is not to imply that as resurrected humans we'll be like God, for we will still operate within boundaries of his creation. But it suggests that the freedom that will allow us to utilize our gifting will free us to pursue his wider creation.

Set free in God's universe we will love as we want, for that will be as he wants. God desires that his children live within the perfection and wholeness he intended in the first creation. Daniel the prophet opens the curtains on this in his prediction, "Those who are wise will shine like the brightness of the heavens, and those who lead many to righteousness, like the stars for ever and ever" (Dan. 12:3). Interestingly, Jesus picks up Daniel's line as he concludes his parable on the good seed and the weeds (Matt. 13:43). Such brightness speaks of energy, power, and illumination. And who does it speak of? God's people, those released by his resurrection and who, in everlasting life, will live his life of greatness and creativity.

We don't start all over again in heaven as if there were nothing in the past. As the resurrected body is reunited with the soul, we will live in continuity with who we have been becoming in this life. Our living on earth has enormous significance beyond making choices to love and serve God, though that is the entry point to life beyond. We also bring into our future life that which we became in this life. Mortal life is not incidental to eternal life. It sets it up. What we have become here continues into the life God has prepared for us.

As we work and live, the old "enmity" between humanity and the creation will be resolved. The Genesis warning about not being disobedient is resolved as John, in his vision of the new Jerusalem, saw the tree of life in the city, providing fruit and leaves for the healing of the nations (Rev. 22:1-3). The distinction of good and evil has been obliterated. What divided human life and stewardship, making it "painful toil" (Gen. 3:17) is now the source of physical health and international peacemaking. United with the soil and nature, our work exists in harmony, no longer in tension.

What Will Heaven Look Like?

Will it be a garden or a city? Two of the most powerful symbols used in the Scriptures, one at the beginning and the other at the end, provide opposite views of God's good creation. Genesis provides the first, the Garden of Eden, generally believed to be in southern Iraq by the Euphrates River. "The LORD God took the man and put him in the Garden of Eden to work it and take care of it" (Gen. 2:15). The garden symbolized a harmonious relationship and the perfect world for procreation of human, animal, and vegetable life.

That was in the beginning. At the end of the Bible we read:

I saw the Holy City, the new Jerusalem, coming down out of heaven from God, prepared as a bride beautifully dressed for her husband. And I heard a loud voice from the throne saying, "Now the dwelling of God is with men, and he will live with them. They will be his people, and God himself will be with them and be their God. He will wipe every tear from their eyes. There will be no more death or mourning or crying or pain, for the old order of things has passed away" (Rev. 21:2-4).

WHAT CAN WE KNOW ABOUT HEAVEN?

Jerusalem, for the Hebrews, was Yahweh's place of abode. Jerusalem, then and today, is more than a city for the Jews: it symbolizes the place of God's dwelling. In John's vision, the city, the place of habitation provides us with a picture of life after death. It combines metaphors of garden and city:

> Then the angel showed me the river of the water of life, as clear as crystal, flowing from the throne of God and of the Lamb down the middle of the great street of the city. On each side of the river stood the tree of life, bearing twelve crops of fruit, yielding its fruit every month. And the leaves of the tree are for the healing of the nations (Rev. 22:1-2).

Civilization in the new earth will engage with all that is good: rivers, cultivated fields, a city of social intercourse, and peace. The integration of all God's provisions provides those who live there with the incredible vastness of creation.

Will There Be "Time"?

An old gospel song speaks of "when the trumpet of the Lord will sound and time will be no more." Because heaven is eternal, the frequent assumption is that time will not be part of its makeup. However, there is no biblical basis for such an assumption. Though night will be overtaken by constant day, that is not to say that there will not be a sequencing of events, one after the other. John's revelation suggests that events will occur in the new creation. For that to be, some sort of time element must exist. John describes the tree of life as "yielding its fruit every month" (Rev. 22:2). There is a sense that in heaven we will be aware of the quality and quantity of time even though it may be an everlasting present in which time is stretched out with no past or future.[44]

105

What Can We Take with Us?

In a parable (Luke 16:19-31) Jesus challenged our narrow thinking on what really matters. In the parable two men die: a rich man and Lazarus, a beggar covered with sores who came each day to the rich man's gate for food. In the afterlife the rich man is in torment and Lazarus is basking in the presence of God. The stark contrast of these two shows that what we carry from this life to the next is not the same as what we consider important in this life. Matthew records Jesus' teaching on the same subject:

> Do not store up for yourselves treasures on earth, where moth and rust destroy, and where thieves break in and steal. But store up for yourselves treasures in heaven, where moth and rust do not destroy, and where thieves do not break in and steal (Matt. 6:19-20).

This invites the question: "What can I carry into the new creation that could be construed as being 'treasure'"? The word triggers thoughts of a healthy bank account, equity in real estate, a pension plan, or articles a culture deems valuable. However, we don't need a mortician, financial planner, or theologian to help us understand that none of that kind of treasure goes with us.

What we take into eternity is ourselves and the good done for others, who in turn bring that into the new creation. Jesus' call to store up treasure is generally interpreted to mean that our investment is only what we do for others. But that ignores our own reality. The person I am becoming is one in whom the creator has invested his image. To understand this is not to inflate self but simply to remind us what treasure and investment mean. Because the quality of my life here transfers into everlasting life, the quality of who I am becoming now matters greatly to who I'll be there.

Life is a gift. What we have now continues into life forever. To assume that a loving God will pretend that what we became here doesn't flow into the future is to disregard the nature of creation. The treasure invested in our own persons will be ongoing in that new creation.

Peter, in speaking about the day when the Lord will inaugurate his new heavens and new earth, asks a question: "Since everything will be destroyed in this way [that is, by fire], what kind of people ought you to be? You ought to live holy and godly lives as you look forward to the day of God and speed its coming" (2 Peter 3:11-12). The goodness and quality of our earthly lives has resonance in the new creation which is why life is so critical, and not merely a time in which we are "just a-passin' through."

Will I Know Everything?

If we've ever thought life was about learning, we haven't even begun to learn. Heaven is not about knowing everything; it's a place in which we know that knowing is not diminished by fragmentary evidence or forgotten promises. Universities that populate this new world will serve without narrow bias. Development of ingenious machines to serve the wider agenda of God's unlimited worlds will emerge from minds no longer reined in by human frailties and anxieties. We will be better suited to see that because all of life comes from God, we are all called on to serve the good. That alone will take the roof off our ability to be creative and productive. The power of heaven is that it's a magnet of hope, pulling people who live in the lowest of times toward living in the best of times. It becomes the bedrock of faith that for everyone who chooses, heaven awaits. Pain and despair are temporary. Heaven's not.

Writer Philip Yancey puts it this way:

> The Bible never belittles human disappointment, but it does add one key word: temporary. What we feel now, we will not always feel. Our disappointment is itself a sign, an aching, a hunger for something better. And faith is, in the end, a kind of homesickness—for a home we have never visited but have never once stopped longing for.[45]

Heaven becomes the last chapter. In spite of disaster and failure, life can be wrapped into God's forever. The darkness of not being able to find answers to the "whys" of life is rolled back. No longer will God be hidden. Job, in all of his tragic inquiries, seeking answers to the catastrophes of his life, blurted out, "in my flesh I will see God; I myself will see him with my own eyes!" (19:26)

Heaven is a real place where those accepted by Christ will live. It's a place where life is lived on a physical planet, where recreation and work aren't opposites as they are for us today. A world where learning will leap the barriers of our current restrictions, and the pain of our failures and sufferings of our fallenness will be over. Heaven is for those who want it.

Eight

WHAT HAPPENS BETWEEN DEATH AND RESURRECTION?

> Our lifelong nostalgia, our longing to be reunited with some-
> thing in the universe from which we now feel cut off, to be
> on the inside of some door which we have always seen from
> the outside, is not mere neurotic fancy, but the truest index of
> our real situation. And to be summoned inside would be both
> glory and honor beyond all our merits and also the healing of
> that old ache.
>
> C.S. Lewis, The Weight of Glory

When Jim Chapman went public with his story of a near-death
experience, interest in his daily talk show shot up. People were
interested in what had happened to him in the moment of
death: some were frightened, others fascinated. The absolute
unknown of what happens the instant our hearts stop beating, combined with miscellaneous information we've gathered from our culture about what people *think* happens, can
be scary. Will I meet Jesus or will it be Satan? Will I end up in
heaven or in hell? Will I float or walk? Will I get a reward or be
punished? The questions stimulate both interest and anxiety.

For Christians, the critical point after death is the return
of Jesus to earth, at which time those, both dead and alive,
who believe in him, are given eternal, resurrected bodies and
an eternal home in heaven. We now turn to the question of
what happens to those who have died before his return: what
happens to them during this time gap between dying and

receiving a resurrected body? What happens to them as they await this next major moment?

This period of transition between death and resurrection is what we know least about. Old Testament writers were more concerned about the community of Israel and its survival than they were about individuals. The New Testament makes occasional references to this interim time, just enough for us to draw some reasonable conclusions. The door is just slightly ajar, allowing us to see that in this period we are conscious of self, others, and God.

There are two primary views about our state between death and resurrection: "soul sleep," in which the soul goes into an unconscious state, and consciousness, in which the person is aware of what is going on.

The argument that this period is a time of soul sleep comes from texts that explicitly speak about the dead being asleep. In the Old Testament the psalmist noted, "It is not the dead who praise the Lord, those who go down to silence" (Ps. 115:17). King Solomon, in his search for meaning, wrote, "the dead know nothing" (Ecc. 9:5). In the New Testament, when Jesus was told of the death of his good friend Lazarus, he said, "Our friend Lazarus has fallen asleep; but I am going there to wake him up" (John 11:11). Upon hearing that, the disciples advised that if he would be left alone, he would awaken. To clear up any misconceptions about Lazarus' state, Jesus said, "Lazarus is dead," and commanded Lazarus to come out of the tomb. John records, "The dead man came out, his hands and feet wrapped with strips of linen, and a cloth around his face" (John 11:44).

Other texts that speak of being asleep include the incident of Stephen, a leader in the early church, who was stoned to death. Luke records, "He fell asleep" (Acts 7:60). Paul, in writing to Christians, spoke about "those who fall asleep" (1 Thess. 4:13–

15). John wrote, "Blessed are the dead who die in the Lord . . . they will rest from their labor" (Rev. 14:13).

Do these references mean that people in transition are therefore asleep, meaning unconscious? I think not. The term *sleep* is an apt one, giving us the sense that this period is a time of rest, a prelude before the next stage of eternal life. To interpret this period as one of literal sleep, waiting for resurrection in an unconscious transitional state, does not fit with what seems to be a pattern of New Testament texts, which is that for Christians there is an immediate transition into the presence of Christ. It seems more consistent with the biblical texts to view this interim period as one in which we are conscious, aware of our selves, our past, the surroundings, and the important implications our earthly life has on everlasting life.

In a conversation between Jesus and a criminal as they hung on adjacent crosses, the criminal asked Jesus to remember him when "you come into your kingdom." Jesus responded, "I tell you the truth, today you will be with me in paradise" (Luke 23:43). Though the criminal was not given an exemption to bypass death, Jesus made it clear that following death he would consciously exist in a place ruled by Christ.

In the Revelation "the souls of those who had been slain . . . called out in a loud voice, 'How long, Sovereign Lord, holy and true, until you judge the inhabitants of the earth and avenge our blood?'" (Rev. 6:9-10).

The Apostle Paul speaks about being in one of two places, "to be away from the body and at home with the Lord" (2 Cor. 5:8). This suggests that being at home with the Lord is a state of consciousness, for a person who is asleep would not be aware of being with the Lord.

In the text concerning the martyr Stephen, the historian Luke notes that before he "fell asleep"—while he was being stoned—he said, "I see heaven open and the Son of Man standing at the right hand of God" (Acts 7:56). For Stephen to see his coming place and then to be unconscious at his arrival there seems disconnected, even though for those who saw him die, his obvious condition was not unlike sleep.

However, the most important set of clues about this interim state comes from Jesus' parable concerning a rich man and a beggar named Lazarus.

There was a rich man who was dressed in purple and fine linen and lived in luxury every day. At his gate was laid a beggar named Lazarus, covered with sores and longing to eat what fell from the rich man's table. Even the dogs came and licked his sores.

The time came when the beggar died and the angels carried him to Abraham's side. The rich man also died and was buried. In hell, where he was in torment, he looked up and saw Abraham far away, with Lazarus by his side, so he called to him, "Father Abraham, have pity on me and send Lazarus to dip the tip of his finger in water and cool my tongue, because I am in agony in this fire."

But Abraham replied, "Son, remember that in your lifetime you received your good things, while Lazarus received bad things, but now he is comforted here and you are in agony. And besides all this, between us and you a great chasm has been fixed, so that those who want to go from here to you cannot, nor can anyone cross over from there to us."

He answered, "Then I beg you, father, send Lazarus to my father's house, for I have five brothers. Let him warn them, so that they will not also come to this place of torment."

Abraham replied, "They have Moses and the Prophets; let them listen to them."

"No, father Abraham," he said, "but if someone from the dead goes to them, they will repent."

He said to him, "If they do not listen to Moses and the Prophets, they will not be convinced even if someone rises from the dead" (Luke 16:19-31).

Not surprisingly, Jesus uses a parable to help those listening to him understand principles of life. This form was especially effective in an oral age when people listened to learn rather than read to learn. A story is always layered with local meaning, meanings that are understood only when the hearer understands the subtlety of the imagery and words. As one raised in a farming community of western Canada, I know that stories told among farmers won't easily be understood by stockbrokers.

Reading this story some two thousand years later, one must examine it to understand what Jesus was trying to get across. In reading any of Jesus' parables we ask, what did those who heard it understand within their Jewish and Middle Eastern context?

Jesus gives the beggar the name *Lazarus*, which is a Greek word from the Hebrew meaning, "God has helped." In contrast to the living faith of this poor, sick man we are introduced to the rich man, who was not only insensitive to Lazarus lying at his gate but had no time for God. Jesus here creates two characters who, as opposites, provide a framework from which Jesus teaches.

Here is what this story tells us.

1. There is a continuation of the life of the soul. The nonphysical side of human life is kept from decay. No one need fear that in death our thinking, feeling, and volitional dimension of life dies. As the body dies, the soul is held by Christ. (We learn elsewhere that the soul is waiting to be reunited with the body in resurrection.) Jesus makes it clear that the soul lives on after death, even as the body dies and decays.

2. The location of the soul is under the watchful care of Abraham the Patriarch. It is the "God of Abraham, Isaac, and Jacob" who brought into existence man and woman and sustains them within his care and protection.

3. The soul retains self-awareness. We have no other biblical indication that during this interim period souls can speak, let alone yell across a chasm between Abraham's side and hell. The point here is that the person understands that life choices make a difference in where we end up after death.

4. The dichotomy of comfort and discomfort forewarns us that there is a consequence to how we live out our life on earth. Those found guilty of turning aside from God's offer of life and of living wickedly will experience the discomfort of the place called *Hades*, or hell. These references to both a good and a horrible state are very real.

While this story is helpful in pointing out that life continues in a conscious mode, the New Testament provides us with other insights to assist us in framing our understanding of this time of transition between death and resurrection.

The single most important indicator that we continue to live with consciousness during the transition period is the indwelling life of the Spirit. Those who have chosen to follow Christ become the recipients of the Holy Spirit. Paul, writing to the Christians in Rome, made it clear that by faith the Spirit lives in our bodies while on earth: "You, however, are controlled not by the sinful nature but by the Spirit, if the Spirit of God lives in you. And if anyone does not have the Spirit of Christ, he does not belong to Christ" (Rom. 8:9). In conversion, as the person reaches out in faith to accept the gift of life, the Holy Spirit of God takes up residence in the person. This is what is often referred to as being "born again" or "born from above." The Spirit begins the process of remaking the person, shaping them into the life of Christ.

With this gift of his Spirit resident in us, at death is it lost? We know that the body degenerates into dust, but what about the "inner" self or the soul? Is it abandoned by the Spirit? Paul uses the legal term to describe the significance of the indwelling Spirit. "The Spirit [is given] as a deposit, guaranteeing what is to come" (2 Cor. 5:5). The King James Version uses the word *earnest*, a word borrowed from commercial transaction. For example, when buying a house, one is required to make a deposit to secure its eventual purchase. The term for this deposit is the *earnest*. It is a commitment on the part of the purchaser to later fulfill the obligation of purchasing the house. The Holy Spirit is God's "earnest," or deposit, to secure our future immortality. It would be inconsistent for the Spirit to abandon us in death. Since we know that we receive resurrected bodies at the time of the return of Christ, this gap between death and resurrection is not a time we would be forsaken by God.

Though great mystery surrounds our understanding of how the soul can exist without the body, there is no other way to explain our state of being except that the "soul" portion of the person continues to live in a protected world, overseen by God.

Some suggest that those who have died can see or communicate with those of us still living on the earth. Though this may give comfort in times of grief, there is no biblical evidence that a person in this waiting period is aware of what is going on on earth; nor is there any suggestion that they can communicate with us.

The mystery of our own personhood is made even more mysterious in this discussion of the nature of our being between death of the body and physical resurrection. The problem is this, given that the person is made up of body and soul, what is the nature of the person when the body is decayed and the soul continues to exist in this interim state? There is little information in either testaments on this. The story of the rich man and Lazarus does make it clear that both are in a conscious state, Lazarus being in the protection of God and the rich man now residing in Hades. What we can conclude is that our dead body awaits Christ's return and the accompanied physical resurrection which in uniting with the soul brings us to our eternal state, be it in heaven or hell.

The sequence of events beginning with death seems to be as follows:

- the body dies.
- the soul transits into God's protection, awaiting the return of Christ to earth and resurrection.
- the bodies of both "the righteous and unrighteous" are resurrected and reunited with their souls.
- the judgment of God is given, in which all will give account of their lives.
- each person is assigned to their place of everlasting life.

When I die, my body will decay and my reasoning, consciousness, will, and feelings—what we call soul—will go into God's protective custody with the promise that the entire self will rise at the time of the return of Jesus Christ. At that moment of his return the entire composite of my self will be resurrected and receive the gift of everlasting life.

Again from the parable of Lazarus we learn that the souls accepted by Christ are held in his protective custody. As to those who have not been liberated by Christ and those the Scriptures call "wicked," we know only that they too are conscious, already experiencing the consequence of their choices.

Those who die as believers are now in Christ, waiting for the resurrection. The promise of resurrection is not only the pulsating draw of the message of Christ, but it signifies that the afterlife will be the connecting of body and soul so that we can enjoy the life brought by God's creation, eternally and whole.

Nine

IS HELL A REAL PLACE?

I willingly believe that the damned are, in one sense, successful, rebels to the end; that the doors of hell are locked on the
inside. . . . They enjoy forever the horrible freedom they have
demanded, and are therefore self-enslaved: just as the blessed,
forever submitting to obedience, become through all eternity
more and more free.

C.S. Lewis, *The Problem of Pain*

There are questions that trouble us about the idea of hell,
such as, how could a God of love create a place of everlasting punishment? Yet, even though people ask the question,
there continues to be a rather strong belief in the reality of hell.
Gallup Polls conducted between 1992 and 1999 indicate that
79 percent of Americans believe there will be a day when God
judges whether you go to heaven or hell.[46] A survey by George
Barna in 1996 found that 69 percent of Americans believe in
hell, though they are divided on whether it is a physical location (31 percent) or a state of separation from the presence of
God (37 percent).[47]

Writing about hell is unpleasant at the best of times. Today's
mood of political correctness makes it downright offensive.
We live in an age in which spirituality is a hot topic and religion fascinates people from all walks of life, but a predomi-
nant breed of pluralism contends that varying viewpoints are
to exist in equal validity side by side, and any view that claims
to be based on absolute truth doesn't deserve the right to be
stated. In philosophy one can tout any number of theories,

just as long as you don't assert that one may be true. Moral debates consume enormous amounts of public media time, but a debater had better not say that Jesus is the only way.

How much easier it is to anticipate the beauty and freedom of heaven than to speak about the pain and bondage of hell. How much easier to surmise that hell is only a metaphor than to conclude from the biblical text that it's real. We allow all sorts of views, but when it comes to this subject, someone who believes in hell is usually accused of narrowness and bigotry. But not to press forward and honestly examine what the Bible says would be to fall victim to half-truths. Eternity is not to be trifled with. The stakes are too high to set aside this part of the future life just because it is discomforting and unpleasant.

To try to describe hell is not unlike describing heaven: both require human and earthbound words, images, and metaphors that describe a location, not a state of mind. Hell as a subject has been given various treatments, be it Dante's *Divine Comedy* or Milton's *Paradise Lost*. Each summer I read C.S. Lewis'— the grand Oxford storyteller—*The Great Divorce*, in which he takes us on a journey from hell to heaven. Along the way he encounters ghosts from hell who try to talk him into staying there and meets redeemed spirits from heaven who help him understand the world of heaven. Though he makes no attempt to describe hell in classic biblical fashion, he lifts us from seeing only the literalness with which we usually envision hell to see the factors that drive people to choose hell.[48]

It begins as the narrator, alone in the darkness of early evening, stands in the rain at a bus stop in a dingy part of town where no one seems to live. The only people he can see are at the bus stop, and so he joins them, even though they all seem to be bad-tempered, nasty, and forever quarreling with each other.

The storyteller is taken aback when one of those waiting for the bus speaks about his death in the past tense as if it had already taken place. He soon comes to learn that the Grey Town of empty houses is the result of people getting what they want. The millions of miles of houses are empty because as people become annoyed with their neighbors, they wish for another house and in that instant get what they want. Driven by uninhibited desires, their wishes are met. For in hell, as he observed, one gets what one wants. Because of their alienation from God, those in hell are also alienated from each other. As the story continues we learn that everyone can make the transition from hell to heaven if they choose, but for various reasons those who made the trip to heaven to check it out, all reject it and return to hell in the Grey Town.

While Lewis' insight into the nature of life in hell opens our thinking to imagine living in a world without God, one must not conclude from his story that hell is only a rather gloomy and uncomfortable place. In biblical language hell is more than that: it's a place where evil is at work, "where their worm does not die, and the fire is not quenched" (Mark 9:48).

In moving from Lewis' story line, which opens our minds to the "logic" of why people choose hell, we come to the actual text of the two testaments to see what is said about its nature. As we do so, it will be helpful to first clarify the words the Bible uses.

In the Old Testament, the Hebrew word *Sheol* denotes the place to which all go at death. According to the Hebrew Testament everyone, whether good or bad, is assigned to the world of the dead. The Psalmist wrote, "What man can live and not see death, or save himself from the power of the grave [*Sheol*]?" (Ps. 89:48). David the King said, "you will not abandon me to the grave [*Sheol*]" (Ps. 16:10). Jacob, having heard what he thought was a report of the death of his son Joseph, said, "in mourning will I go down to the grave [*Sheol*] to my son" (Gen. 37:35).

The Jews had no definite view of the nature or state of *Sheol* or what the soul experienced there. They saw death as the time when men and women descended to a place beneath the earth, which they called *Sheol*. *Sheol* not only denoted *grave* but included the idea of death being a place as well as a state. In *Sheol* the person retained consciousness, as suggested by Isaiah's description of people rousing themselves to meet the King of Babylon (Isa. 14:9-10). What seems to be most important is that *Sheol* as a state of the dead was not the end of human existence. For King David, *Sheol* was not the final word: "because you will not abandon me to the grave [*Sheol*], nor will you let your Holy One see decay. You have made known to me the path of life; you will fill me with joy in your presence, with eternal pleasures at your right hand" (Ps. 16:10-11).

In the New Testament the Hebrew *Sheol* becomes *Hades* in Greek, from which we get the English word *hell*. In English translations *hell* comes from three Greek words:

- *Hades*, used ten times, describes the place of the unrighteous between death and judgment;
- *Gehenna*, used twelve times, describes the final place of the unrighteous after judgment;
- *Tartarus*, used only once, is described as the place fallen angels are confined before they face judgment (2 Peter 2:4).

Hades meant the abode of the unrighteous between death and resurrection as in the story of Lazarus and the rich man. In the Revelation both death and Hades are cast into the lake of fire which originally was reserved for wicked spirits.

The word *Gehenna* comes from Ge-Hinnom, or the land of Hinnom, a valley located just south of Jerusalem. In Old Testament times a "high place"—a place where sacrifices, including those of children, were offered to pagan gods—had been built (Jer. 19:1-6). At its top was a deep hole in which wood was placed, then set on fire by brimstone coming out of the earth. During Jesus' time it was used as a garbage disposal; as people went by they would look down into the valley and see brimstone burning up refuse. Jesus used this valley to symbolize the eternal abode of the wicked. It was a powerful and contemporary metaphor for the place of the unrighteous. Its history gave it color, and its flames and rising smoke provided a picture.

However, because "hell" is so loosely and freely used today it becomes quite confusing. The Bible designates Hades as the place the wicked (unrighteous) go as they await resurrection and judgment. After the judgment those not given eternal life with God are sent to *Gehenna*, the final abode of the unrighteous. So to avoid confusion I'll use the designation *hell* to mean Gehenna, the final place of punishment.

To assist us in seeing how the New Testament treats this subject, we'll look at Jesus' descriptions, the Apostle Paul's explanations of who are guilty, and John's dramatic pictures in the Revelation, depicting life at the end of time.

Jesus' Teaching

Jesus' primary way of teaching was by parable. He was particularly skilled in storytelling. Using this technique, and by taking examples from local life, he spoke in language both plain and colorful to convey his core ideas. For us today, however, trying to put together his words through the records of four writers, it is not always easy to ascertain who will end up in hell and for what reasons. That's why it is important to allow the entire text of the New Testament to examine this concept of hell. It is only as we link Jesus' teaching with the subsequent works of Paul and John that a picture of this place and time become more clear.

Apart from using terms such as *fire, punishment,* and *eternal fire,*

Jesus doesn't provide much description. Nor does he follow up by giving an explanation of what these words mean. In the parable of the rich man and Lazarus, the rich man is in obvious discomfort as he says he is "in agony in this fire." Though it isn't clear what this specifically means, it does signal that this man, whom Jesus judges as deserving of punishment, is in a place of great suffering.

The severity of hell is reinforced by Jesus warning people not to be trapped by protecting their sin. He uses this physical analogy:

> If your hand or your foot causes you to sin cut it off and throw it away. It is better for you to enter life maimed or crippled than to have two hands or two feet and be thrown into eternal fire. And if your eye causes you to sin, gouge it out and throw it away. It is better for you to enter life with one eye than to have two eyes and be thrown into the fire of hell (Matt. 18:8-9).

Nowhere is Jesus explicit about the nature of hell. He does, however, make it clear that at some moment there will be a judgment in which some will be sent to a place of great discomfort and punishment. In a parable to the disciples about the kingdom, he describes the dividing of people in which the wicked will be sorted out from the righteous. He uses an image of fishermen pulling in their nets filled with all sorts of fish and, once on land, sorting through their catch, throwing away the bad and keeping the good. Jesus follows up his story with an explanation:

> This is how it will be at the end of the age. The angels will come and separate the wicked from the righteous and throw them into the fiery furnace, where there will be weeping and gnashing of teeth (Matt. 13:49-50).

123

John the Baptist, Jesus' cousin and the one who announced him to that world, said,

I baptize you with water for repentance. But after me will come one who is more powerful than I, whose sandals I am not fit to carry. He will baptize you with the Holy Spirit and with fire. His winnowing fork is in his hand, and he will clear his threshing floor, gathering his wheat into the barn and burning up the chaff with unquenchable fire (Matt. 3:11-12).

In this pronouncement, John said Jesus would do more than give great messages of hope and forgiveness—he would also distinguish between the good and bad. This theme is picked up in Jesus' parables, in which he identifies three groups who will be punished (Matt. 25).

In a story of ten wedding attendants, five prepare themselves by filling their lamps so that when the bridegroom arrives they will be ready. To those who dawdled away their time, and in the end bang on the door to be admitted because they failed to be ready, the groom responds, "I tell you the truth, I don't know you" (Matt. 25:12). The suggestion is that heaven is only for those who prepare for it. Those who throw away their opportunities end up in a place other than heaven.

Jesus continues with a most remarkable story of a business operator who, before going on a journey, entrusts various amounts of money to three of his employees. On his return he finds that the first, to whom he gave five talents, has invested the funds and doubled them. The second, who had been given two talents, also doubled the money. To both the master responds, "Well done, good and faithful servant! You have been faithful with a few things; I will put you in charge of many things. Come and share your master's happiness!"

IS HELL A REAL PLACE?

Then he turns to the one who had been given one talent, who seems intent on defending his action. "'Master,' he said, 'I knew that you are a hard man, harvesting where you have not sown and gathering where you have not scattered seed. So I was afraid and went out and hid your talent in the ground. See, here is what belongs to you.'"

You can hear the owner explode:

You wicked, lazy servant! So you knew that I harvest where I have not sown and gather where I have not scattered seed? Well then, you should have put my money on deposit with the bankers, so that when I returned I would have received it back with interest. Take the talent from him and give it to the one who has the ten talents. For everyone who has will be given more, and he will have an abundance. Whoever does not have, even what he has will be taken from him. And throw that worthless servant outside, into the darkness, where there will be weeping and gnashing of teeth (Matt. 25:26-30).

The third example Jesus uses is the separating of the sheep and goats. He identifies the difference in terms of their behavior toward the unfortunate—the hungry, the homeless, the sick, the prisoners.

In speaking to the sheep (who treated the unfortunate with compassion and generosity) he says, "Come, you who are blessed by my Father; take your inheritance, the kingdom prepared for you since the creation of the world. For I was hungry and you gave me something to eat, I was thirsty and you gave me something to drink, I was a stranger and you invited me in, I needed clothes and you clothed me, I was sick and you looked after me, I was in prison and you came to visit me (Matt. 25:34-36)." He then turns to the goats (who did none of those things) with these devastating words, "Depart from me, you who are cursed, into the eternal fire prepared for the devil and his angels" (25:41).

Then the Scripture continues: "Then they will go away to eternal punishment, but the righteous to eternal life" (25:46).

What we learn from Jesus' teachings is that there will be a dividing of people, and those he judges to be wicked will be sent to a place of punishment.

In addition to these parables, Jesus makes a considerable number of references to who ends up in hell. He taught that in his kingdom issues such as "hating" were seen as being the same as murder, and lusting as adultery. He gives this warning:

You have heard that it was said to the people long ago, "Do not murder, and anyone who murders will be subject to judgment." But I tell you that anyone who is angry with his brother will be subject to judgment. Again, anyone who says to his brother, "Raca ['you empty head!']," is answerable to the Sanhedrin [the Jerusalem city council dominated by Jewish religious leaders]. But anyone who says, "You fool!" will be in danger of the fire of hell (Matt. 5:21-22).

What he ends up doing is including us all as guilty of punishment, for surely none can claim to have committed no sins of hate, lust, or greed.

Surprisingly, Jesus doesn't use hell as being the place where those in the seamier side of society end up. In fact, his specific references are directed to his disciples and religious leaders. Matthew records that in a remarkable moment of responding to the faith of a Roman soldier, Jesus launched into a stinging rebuke to his own followers. Many religious leaders, he said, will come to the feast, but many "will be thrown outside, into the darkness, where there will be weeping and gnashing of teeth (Matt. 8:12)."

In using some of his strongest language of condemnation on the Pharisees—a Jewish sect concerned about preserving the Hebrew culture from the incursion of the powerful Greek culture of Hellenism—Jesus speaks in particularly harsh terms:

> Woe to you, teachers of the law and Pharisees, you hypocrites! You travel over land and sea to win a single convert, and when he becomes one, you make him twice as much a son of hell as you are (Matt. 23:15).
>
> You snakes! You brood of vipers! How will you escape being condemned to hell? (23:33)

For Jesus, hell is not a place particularly reserved for the worst perpetrators of evil. He taught that sin is not only that which violates the moral code, *but a spirit that rejects God as creator and attempts to live as if one doesn't need God.* This going it alone is a life of unfaith in which God is seen as irrelevant and unnecessary. Jesus makes this clear in a conversation he had with a religious leader, Nicodemus.

This learned and respected man came to Jesus asking how he could become part of God's kingdom. To this intellectual sophisticate, Jesus answers, "No one can enter the kingdom of God unless he is born of water and the Spirit" (John 3:5). As they continue in conversation, Jesus gives Nicodemus the heart message of his coming: "For God so loved the world that he gave his one and only Son, that whoever believes in him shall not perish but have eternal life" (3:16). One who believes is exempt from punishment, which is to say that those who do not believe do not experience God's provision of eternal life and go into eternal death.

WHAT HAPPENS WHEN I DIE?

In our freedom we choose. That is the nature of eternal life. C.S. Lewis reminds us that the doors of hell are locked on the inside.[49] As Adam and Eve made their choice, so we inevitably make ours. We often ask, "What about those who aren't old enough, cogent enough, or in a position to make a choice?" Those questions won't let us off the hook. As Lewis tells it, those lost in eternity are those who enjoy forever the horrible freedom they have demanded. He suggests that we are divided into two groups: those who say, "Thy will be done," and those to whom God finally says, "Thy will be done." This freedom to choose is synonymous with wanting to go our own way. Biblical freedom is counter-cultural in that freedom is defined as unfettered opportunities to obey God, not the right to disobey. Obedience leads, in an upside-down way, to freedom, while disobedience, camouflaged by a sense of independence, leads to bondage and a loss of freedom.

On the matter of judgment, we are called to consider the frightful option of being judged not worthy of Jesus' heaven. Those who hear the scary words "I don't know you or where you come from. Away from me, all you evildoers!" (Luke 13:27) will receive the destiny they chose. For each of us there are opportunities during life to make choices toward God. But in that day when those who have chosen to live apart from Christ—as did the rich man in the parable of Lazarus—and wake up to see the enormous mistake they've made, it will be too late. There will be no further opportunity to reverse the choices of a lifetime.

The Apostle Paul's Teachings

It is to the Apostle Paul we turn next to help us make sense of this subject. In probably the most important letter he wrote, Paul in writing to the Christians in Rome, paints a dark picture of the decay of human moral life. Note his list of the unrighteous and wicked who deserve death, or hell:

They have become filled with every kind of wickedness, evil, greed and depravity. They are full of envy, murder, strife, deceit and malice. They are gossips, slanderers, God-haters, insolent, arrogant and boastful; they invent ways of doing evil; they disobey their parents; they are senseless, faithless, heartless, ruthless. Although they know God's righteous decree that those who do such things deserve death, they not only continue to do these very things but also approve of those who practice them (Rom. 1:29-32).

Note his list doesn't stop with murders but includes those who gossip as well. No person is exempt. The Old Testament law had been given to help the Jews to live righteous lives, but Paul concludes that even with the help of this law, all are still guilty. In the end, whether we destroy by murder or by gossip, we are all guilty. Lifting a line from King David (Ps. 14:3), Paul warns us, "there is no one who does good, not even one" (Rom. 3:12). He continues, "for all have sinned and fall short of the glory of God" (3:23). So it is not only those whom society considers "bad" whose destination is eternal "lostness." Paul here joins with Jesus in making it clear that *the definition of evil is so wide as to include everyone.* We tend to assume that those who pay their taxes, don't beat their children or spouses and are, in general, good people, will be okay in eternity, believing that it's our good deeds and reasonableness that gain us entry. As good as those are, they aren't sufficient reasons when confronted with the question, "Why should you be given access to God's eternal world?"

Paul reduces us all to the common denominator of the unrighteous: "All have sinned and fall short of the glory of

God" (Rom. 3:23). As good as we may have been, "all our righteous acts are like filthy rags" (Isa. 64:6). Our inclination is to size up our lives like a checklist of good deeds. We assume that if our good deeds outweigh our bad, we'll be admitted to heaven.

The gospel cuts the issue differently. We do bad because by nature we are bad. Hell is not for those who are more bad than others. Though we may perceive some as being better or worse than others, eternal death is our common destiny because we are creatures "sinful at birth, sinful from the time my mother conceived me" (Ps. 51:5). Our very best doesn't overcome that evil which has been inherited by the original fall. By this measuring stick each of us is guilty and not deserving of heaven.

There is a question as to the resurrection of both the "righteous" and "unrighteous." Paul, in preaching to Felix, said "there will be a resurrection of both the righteous and the wicked" (Acts 24:15). These two resurrections are:

1. The "righteous" receive bodies in which they live out their everlasting life,
2. The resurrection of the "unrighteous" results in judgment, after which they receive eternal punishment.

"To those who by persistence in doing good seek glory, honor and immortality, he will give eternal life. But for those who are self-seeking and who reject the truth and follow evil, there will be wrath and anger" (Rom. 2:7-8).

"He will punish those who do not know God and do not obey the gospel of our Lord Jesus. They will be punished with everlasting destruction and shut out from the presence of the Lord and from the majesty of his power" (2 Thes. 1:8-9).

The actual embodiment of the person judged for eternal death is unclear. We are not told the actual physical dimension of those judged to be eternally lost. This is in contrast to those who in heaven live their eternal life in resurrected bodies which have been unified at the return of Christ.[50]

John: The Revelation

There are many views on how to interpret the Revelation by John the seer. This fascinating vision deals primarily with messages to seven churches, describing what will take place at the end of the world and in the place of God's heaven. We want to avoid getting caught up in the myriad renderings of what the various metaphors and symbols represent. Instead we look for what helps us learn about the nature of hell and who is sent there. John uses the word *torment* to convey a sense of enormous discomfort. He describes those who serve the Antichrist: "If anyone worships the beast . . . and receives his mark on the forehead . . . he too, will drink of the wine of God's fury . . . He will be tormented with burning sulfur . . . And the smoke of their torment rises for ever and ever" (Rev. 14:9-11).

He describes a sequence of events that begins at the time of judgment:

Then I saw a great white throne and him who was seated on it. Earth and sky fled from his presence, and there was no place for them. And I saw the dead, great and small, standing before the throne, and books were opened. Another book was opened, which is the book of life. The dead were judged according to what they had done as recorded in the books. The sea gave up the dead that were in it, and death and Hades gave up the dead that were in them, and each person was judged according to what he had done. Then death and

Hades were thrown into the lake of fire. The lake of fire is the second death. If anyone's name was not found written in the book of life, he was thrown into the lake of fire (Rev. 20:11–15).

At judgment we all will be faced with our past. John says that those whose names are not recorded in the "book of life" will end up in the "lake of fire." This phrase is one used by Paul: "I ask you, loyal yokefellow, help these women who have contended at my side in the cause of the gospel, along with Clement and the rest of my fellow workers, whose names are in the book of life" (Phil. 4:3). We don't know the nature of these records. The point is that we are reminded that there are records kept about our lives. To have one's name noted is to say that there is a means whereby we can ensure our names are included so that at judgment we will be recognized and given entry to God's eternal home. John uses it throughout The Revelation:

He who overcomes will, like them, be dressed in white. I will never blot out his name from the book of life, but will acknowledge his name before my Father and his angels (Rev. 3:5).

All inhabitants of the earth will worship the beast—all whose names have not been written in the book of life belonging to the Lamb that was slain from the creation of the world (13:8).

The beast, which you saw, once was, now is not, and will come up out of the Abyss and go to his destruction. The inhabitants of the earth whose names have not been written in the book of life from the creation of the world will be astonished when they see the beast, because he once was, now is not, and yet will come (17:8).

And I saw the dead, great and small, standing before the throne, and books were opened. Another book was opened, which is the book of life. The dead were judged according to what they had done as recorded in the books (20:12).

If anyone's name was not found written in the book of life, he was thrown into the lake of fire (20:15).

Nothing impure will ever enter it, nor will anyone who does what is shameful or deceitful, but only those whose names are written in the Lamb's book of life (21:27).

Through these powerful symbols, John points out that hell is a frightful place where God is absent and where evil is unleashed and unrestrained. It is a place where a moral vacuum of Godlessness dominates. Today we all experience God's goodness, for it rains on the just and unjust. We take these blessings for granted. Not so there.

As with considerations of heaven, we have many questions about hell.

How Long Will it Last?

There are two views on the length of time people sentenced to hell will be there. The traditional view sees judgment as eternal, as is heaven. The other view, called "annihilationism," in short says, "fire and then nothing." That is, after entering the place of judgment, the person ceases to exist. This view is based on four primary considerations.[51]

1. The destruction of the wicked implies that destruction is just that, after which there is no continuing existence. Peter speaks of this by saying that, "the present heavens and earth are reserved for fire, being kept for the day of

judgment and destruction of ungodly men" (2 Peter 3:7).
If the present earth will be renewed, the logic is that hell
will come to an end.

2. God's nature of love is used to argue that a never-ending
   hell seems more like the work of a vindictive God than one
   who, in love, sent his son to pay the cost of human failure.

3. Also, eternal punishment for a person whose lifetime of
   sin was only a few years is a disproportionate amount of
   time. Because God is a just God, then the time of punishment is not eternal.

4. The final argument is that if evil continues in God's
   creation it blemishes the perfect heavens and earth we are
   promised. Termed "cosmological dualism," it contends
   that it is impossible for God to call creation perfect when
   evil exists somewhere in creation.

Though annihilationism is supported by a number of well-
known and respected theologians, most evangelical theologians view the duration of hell as permanent, an everlasting
process, as Paul notes: "He will punish those who do not know
God and do not obey the gospel of our Lord Jesus. They will
be punished with everlasting destruction and shut out from
the presence of the Lord and from the majesty of his power"
(2 Thess. 1:8-9).

Another side to this debate is the Hebrew view of time,
which is more about content than duration. Jesus prayed, "Now
this is eternal life: that they may know you, the only true God,
and Jesus Christ, whom you have sent" (John 17:3). Eternal
life is defined by relationship to God and not by length of time.
Though this doesn't answer the "how long?" question, it does
caution us not to assume that eternity is quantifiably measurable.

Asking the question, "How could a God of love allow
punishment over an eternal span of time?" is the same as asking,

"How could a God of love allow punishment for a short period of time?" The issue isn't "how long?" but "how?"

Regardless of which side one takes in this debate, simply engaging in the question forces us to come to grips with the idea of "lostness" and the frightful situation of being alienated from God.

How Could a God of Love Allow Hell?

There is no more difficult part of the Hebrew and New Testaments than this issue of hell. How much easier it would be to superimpose the love dimension of God over the difficult issues and avoid the matter of his holiness. But as much as the notion of eternal punishment is repugnant, we must not sweep it aside. If we give in to the inclination to focus only on the biblical promises and stories that make us feel good, we transgress its spirit and content.

We live in a moral universe. When a child is sexually molested, tortured, or mutilated there is an instant rising of anger, for we know implicitly that a moral fiber of life has been broken. When a warlord wipes out civilizations, or drug pushers enslave thousands, don't we instinctively insist they meet their judge? Our sense of justice calls for a just judgment. We are moral beings.

A moral universe needs a moral referee. God is at the center of the universe, and thus so is justice. In that sense, hell is a means for moral certitude. However, in our attempt to make sure that the perpetrators of gross immoral deeds—the Hitler-types—are punished, we draw a moral circle to include those who we believe need to be punished, but we draw it so small as to exclude those who have done lesser evils but may deserve to be included. But that is not how Jesus drew the circle. His was much wider. He said, "You have heard that it was said to the

135

people long ago, 'Do not murder, and anyone who murders will be subject to judgment.' But I tell you that anyone who is angry with his brother will be subject to judgment" (Matt. 5:21-22). The issue is that we draw a small circle to define our sense of outrage, forgetting that God's outrage is defined differently. The challenge is to understand that basis on which God draws the circles and not ours.

In our attempt to resolve our sense of God being love with this plan to punish, we may find comfort in knowing that the most evil of offenders will ultimately get what they deserve but end up ignoring the biblical definition of sin. In so doing we fall into the trap of looking for a faith that exempts all except those we think of as the worst. This desire to ensure that the greatest number of people are exempt from eternal judgment is understandable. Our mistake is assuming that moral failure is an issue which affects only us and not God. Moral codes, coming from the designer and implementer of all of life, aren't intended to make us feel good. An ancient word, *holy*, is used to describe God. This isn't a prudish idea designed to keep us from having fun. It deals with the very nature of God. There is a difference between our sense of moral outrage and God's. God does not define good as we do, and what God calls good is not synonymous with the sum total of human happiness. The moral center is not anthropomorphic, finding itself in our humanity; it is theocentric, with its holding point in God.

The ancient Job, battered by loss and bruised by physical distress, asked God to give him an answer for his woes. In his final soliloquy God asks,

Where were you when I laid the earth's foundation? . . . Have you ever given orders to the morning, or shown the dawn its place . . . Have the gates of death been shown to

you . . . Surely you know, for you were already born! You
have lived so many years! (Job 38:4, 12, 17, 21).

Job concludes that we simply can't grasp God's view of
justice: "Surely I spoke of things I did not understand, things
too wonderful for me to know" (42:3).

The matter of judgment from God is more than an appeal-
ing to our sense of moral outrage. There is within the creator
holiness which is not neutralized by love. The essential nature
of God does not marginalize one part of his nature by another.

Is There a Purgatory?

This idea was introduced to the church by Pope Gregory in the
sixth century in a series of works called *Dialogues*. This idea—a
teaching that those who die at peace with the church but who
are less than perfect must go through a time of purification—was
cemented into Roman Catholic theology at the Council of Trent
(1545–63) in reaction to the burgeoning Protestant movement.

Purgatory, as a Catholic doctrine, teaches that there is an
interim between earth and heaven, a time and place to prepare
for heaven. People are punished for their sins and are able to
make amends through penance and receive a status of righteousness with God.

The text used to support the notion of purgatory comes from
2 Maccabees (12:43-45), one of the books written between
the end of the Old Testament and the beginning of the New.
These books are called the Apocrypha. Though never accepted
by the Jews as part of their Scriptures and never included in the
King James Version or other Protestant versions, they continue
to be included in Roman Catholic versions.

The doctrine of purgatory taught that because some sins are
more grievous than others, it will take some people longer than

others to work their way through this period of purgatory. Prayers and masses could enable those in purgatory to move more quickly through their time of purification.

The book describes Judas Maccabee, who led the Jewish army against their enemies. It records that as the Jewish soldiers recovered the bodies of their fallen comrades, they noticed that each of them had a small idol tucked away in his tunic. Concluding this was the reason they had lost their lives, Judas Maccabee encouraged people to go to Jerusalem and make a sacrifice for sin with the hope that by this post-death sacrifice, those who had died would be considered pious. The story ends with this line, "This is why he had this atonement sacrifice offered for the dead, so that they might be released from their sins."

This doctrine is outside what the New Testament tells us is our place at our immediate moment of death. Paul wrote that at death we go into God's presence (Phil. 1:21–24 and 2 Cor. 5:8) with no stops in between. Encountering Christ in death is a moment of great pleasure, while purgatory is something quite different.

Further, the New Testament makes it clear that entrance into heaven is not on the basis of good works but rather by trusting in what Jesus has done: "For it is by grace you have been saved, through faith—and this not from yourselves, it is the gift of God—not by works, so that no one can boast" (Eph. 2:8-9).

How Is One Exempt from Hell?

Jesus came to answer that question. His sacrifice ensures our eternal well-being. The promise that a place is being prepared for us is not a figure of speech. There *is* a place for each of us in the final kingdom of God's rule. The driving force of God's love built the bridge from our current fallenness to his eternal life. God's will is that we bypass eternal judgment and go directly into everlasting life. The thread that weaves its way throughout the entire Bible is faith, which is to put one's life into the hands of God, accepting his act of bringing his Son into life here on earth so that by his death and resurrection we not only receive his life here on earth but the promised everlasting life.

Jesus tells us that our goodness will never satisfy the requirements of a holy and just God. But he didn't leave us there. I repeat his famous words to Nicodemus: "For God so loved the world that he gave his one and only Son, that whoever believes in him shall not perish but have eternal life" (John 3:16). *The way to heaven is not by the good we think we have done, but in believing and trusting in the good Jesus did for us.*

The Apostle Paul provides this prescription to our problem of being judged unrighteous because of our inherent evil: "Therefore, since we have been justified through faith, we have peace with God through our Lord Jesus Christ, through whom we have gained access by faith into this grace in which we now stand. And we rejoice in the hope of the glory of God" (Rom. 5:1-2). We are justified—meaning, judged as if we had never sinned—by the work of Christ, not by our good deeds. It is faith in Christ that gives us entry into heaven.

As a young man in search of meaning, wanting very much to do something of value in life, I came to see that the life Jesus offers was just what I needed. Knowing Christ not only provides the radical change I need today, it also gives me the promise that in the afterlife I will live in his good world. And how can I know? By accepting his gift of eternal life. And *accepting* is the operative word. This gift of faith is available for all. None are excluded.

When I stand before God at the judgment seat, what will be my claim to be invited into God's heaven? There is one

WHAT HAPPENS WHEN I DIE?

simple but profound answer: I have accepted the death of Jesus as payment for my guilt and moral failure. He has canceled my debt and promised me a place in his everlasting world.

While traveling by train from Colombo up the mountains of Sri Lanka to Kandy to speak at a youth conference, I happened to sit next to Father Arnold, head of the local Roman Catholic seminary. After our hours together, he invited me for dinner and then to address his seminarians. A sacred Buddhist shrine, the Temple to the Buddha's Tooth, is located in Kandy. After speaking to the seminarians I invited questions. A young man stood and asked, "How can we as Christians stand on the steps of the temple and tell a father or mother that Jesus is the only way to heaven?"

It was a tough but sincere question. I said, "I serve a loving God who knows not only what is right but what is fair. In my attempts to serve with justice, I know that even in my best moments my justice is far short of what is perfect. When I stand before God the Father at the great judgment seat, his decision will be fair, just, and good. Then I'll see that his ways, far above mine, are good."

Will a child who dies before understanding faith end up in hell? Will someone who has never heard of the gift of Christ be cast into eternal punishment? I can't imagine God doing anything other than that which is fair and just. As much as I try to understand God in his justice, love, and mercy, I fall short of knowing the absolute greatness of his being. In the light of that day, we will see his justice, love, and mercy in incredible dimensions. The fright of hell will be overtaken by the unbelievable goodness of our home in heaven.

Ten

CAN WE HOPE
THROUGH DEATH?

And in the perfect time, O perfect God,
When we are in our home, our natal home,
When joy shall carry every sacred load,
And from its life and peace no heart shall roam,
What if thou make us able to make like thee—
To light with moons, to clothe with greenery,
To hand gold sunsets o'er a rose and purple sea.

George MacDonald, *Diary of an Old Soul*

If Jesus hadn't risen from the dead, the Apostle Paul would have thrown up his hands and said, "Hey, let's go out and party, 'cause folks, this is all there is!"

The reason he doesn't is that Christ's resurrection is proof that life doesn't end at death. For Paul, the physical resurrection of Jesus not only is central to God's activity in human history, but it established the prototype of what we will be after we die. His resurrection is so central to what happens after death that without it, the framework of Christian faith collapses.

Jesus came at a time when the Greco-Roman world cast its shadow over the Middle Eastern world. The message of a king rising from the dead was revolutionary, upsetting the structures and personalities running the world. The announcement of the birth of a king frightened Herod the King so much that he sent soldiers to kill every male under two years of age in Bethlehem. If the very possibility of another king was upsetting, imagine

141

the fear when they heard that it was the Son of God coming as king. This was not just any ordinary rival to Rome's power. The rumor that someone beyond Caesar's control is about to arrive does more than raise anxiety in a politician's heart about being replaced in his position of power; it threatens a death blow to the entire regime.

Promising to be more than just another emperor, this new king posed an alternative to bloodshed. Instead of offering something other than the "ghostly" forces of the Greek underworld and practitioners of magic, Jesus promised to break the power of death itself. The light he promised would drive away the blight and shadow of death, so that in both life and death, there is eternal freedom.

His revolutionary message also went beyond just sound ethical counsel about life, giving empowerment to live the ethical life. His parables gave such profound insight that even the scholars were stunned by his wisdom. But it was his overcoming death that sent shock waves throughout the world. It was one thing to defy the powermongers of the Roman world, but to deny the gods of their culture their rule, to help people overcome their inner demons and walk free reborn with the hope they would live forever, was beyond all imagining.

It is that which the gospel offers. Christ sets us free from the cold grip of death and assuages the stinging loss of someone we love. In having bridged death, he promises that we too can make the crossing and walk into a life that is real, without end.

Jesus' defeat of death takes us back to the time our first parents were seduced by evil. They rejected the creator's instruction which in effect was, "Everything in this created order is for you and is your responsibility, but there is just one thing out of your boundaries." They were disallowed access to the fruit of the tree of the knowledge of good and evil. While we have no information about the tree we expect it stood for obedience and thus became a measuring device to test human creation. It wasn't so much that there was some magic potion in the fruit that, when ingested, would help them understand the difference between good and evil, but that in failing to live in obedience to the creator, they would fall under the rule of the fallen angel, the progenitor of evil, Lucifer. Up to that time (for how many years we don't know), they had known only perfect harmony with the creator and the wider creation, but in taking of the tree they came to understand evil and in partaking of that fruit they came to understand good.

God's response to their willful disobedience was directed not only to the human pair but also to this physical manifestation of evil, the serpent. God's curse was without ambiguity:

Cursed are you above all the livestock
and all the wild animals!
You will crawl on your belly
and you will eat dust
all the days of your life.
And I will put enmity
between you and the woman,
    and between your offspring and hers;
he will crush your head,
    and you will strike his heel (Gen. 3:14-15).

We have here the image of a gardener who drives down with his heel at a venomous snake, crushing its head before it can strike and spew out its poison. However, in time, we learn through the gospel that it's not the heel of some gardener that crushes the serpent's head. Instead it was the offspring of Mary, Jesus: "The God of peace [Jesus] will soon crush Satan under your feet" (Rom. 16:20). This goes beyond a promise about future life; it strikes at the very source of death. So, while Adam and Eve were

143

in the very act of disobedience, the creator pointed forward to when the Redeemer would crush the head of evil and death, not just to reduce its impact but to destroy it forever.

To that the writer of the Hebrews says, "Since the children have flesh and blood, he [Jesus] too shared in their humanity so that by his death he might destroy him who holds the power of death—that is, the devil—and free those who all their lives were held in slavery by their fear of death" (Heb. 2:14-15). The destruction of evil does double duty: death no longer holds ultimate power and our fear of death is broken.

With that backdrop, we turn to see what kind of person Jesus of Nazareth, son of Mary and Joseph, was. The book of John, the last of the four Gospels, opens with powerful imagery in describing Jesus. Employing the Greek word *logos*, translated as "word," the writer dips into his contemporary Greek philosophy in which "the word" is used to mean the ultimate of existence. John uses this to good effect: Jesus is ultimate in creation.

He is more than the impressive Old Testament prophets; he is the very God who in the beginning "was God" and was "with God." To the Hebrew community this constituted a sort of polytheism with God seeming to be more than one. This eventually sorted itself out as the early church came to understand that God is both one and trinity: God the Father, God the Son, and God the Holy Spirit. The Son becomes part of the human race as Jesus of Nazareth. The creator, in seeing his creation polluted, enters the world so as to feel what we feel, see what we see, and walk where we walk. In that way "he is touched by the feeling of our infirmities" and out of his God-being leads us across the chasm of death. Not only is he the messenger, but he is the message. It's one thing to tell people that God cares for them, but it's something else to be that God, to love in tangible ways, and to walk with people on their journey. This is the nature of Jesus who came into our life, our world, our literal humanity, not only to speak the word of God but to be the Word itself.

The Hebrew community had been told in many ways, including the Decalogue (the Ten Commandments), which was a clear outline of God's essential requirements, what their God expected of them. They had in their history both good and bad examples of how to live and treat each other. They had been given clear ethical guidelines as the prophets warned them time and again, making it clear what their God required. Those guidelines and examples were not enough. They obviously needed something *more*.

Jesus entered a world shaped by a people whose view of the afterlife was cloudy at best. It was a society influenced by ideas which assumed from Plato that the soul—not the body—would never die, and from the Stoics that death was a welcome end to a life of suffering. When Jesus arrived on the scene, people were groping for something to help them face brutal death directed by the vicious political will of their adversaries. The message was that the God of the universe had come into life itself and had dealt the finality and immutability of death a crippling blow. This, it seemed, was what the Jewish people were looking for. Countless thousands turned to believe in the Christian faith. This promise that a resurrected body would unite with the everlasting soul heading to eternal life became the magnet of the Christian story that caused people to embrace the teachings of the Christian faith.

This teaching was culturally transforming. Tertullian, in the third century, remarked, "There is no nation indeed which is not Christian." And, "We are but of yesterday and we have filled every place among you—cities, islands, fortresses, towns, marketplaces, the very camp, tribes, companies, palace, senate, forum—we have left nothing to you but the temples of your gods."52

This *more* the Hebrews needed was a life-giving gift that went beyond adherence to additional commandments or extra disciplines. It came from the life of the self-confessed Son of God who, because of who he was, knew what he was talking about. It exceeded, was much larger than, the words or ideas of the message. It went past the modeling of character and goodness. It was the transmission of character and goodness into the lives of those who chose to believe.

When Jesus left the earth, he promised that the Holy Spirit would take up residence within those who followed and believed. This was an incredible departure from any other religious idea—that the God of the universe chooses to take up residence, not just in churches and communities of faith, but within the body and soul of the believer. His living is not just within the church or confined to the recited creeds or experienced rituals. It is within each life of those who choose to receive. That is what Jesus spoke about in his conversation with the Jewish teacher Nicodemus. That which I couldn't do before I now can do, for God has taken up residence. That which controlled my life so that attitudes and actions had become habitual, is broken. That which breaks my spirit by the burden of fear is lifted. That is the *more*.

Why did Jesus come? We have seen that in our early beginnings, human life took a turn from the call of its creator and God set in motion a means that would eventually redeem creation, restoring the relationship with its creator.

Jesus Deals with Evil

But there was another factor, which we in our post-modern thinking find hard to understand. We are in the hands of the God of life, who is perfect. This means that the violation of covenant is something over which God can't just shake his head with a "Sorry guys, too bad. Get on to what's next." There is the matter of both the evil done and the existence of evil. Through this evolving relationship of God with the Hebrew community it became evident that a payment was required for the sins of the people, not just as a symbol or ceremony but to satisfy what was rooted in the very character of God. Their sins were more than just an annoyance or inconvenience. They rubbed raw the character of God.

We are prone to see only the loving side of God's character and conveniently ignore his judicial nature. Justice requires offsetting the wrong with the right. For God there is no way of avoiding or ignoring the sin of his creation. And how was that sin to be faced? In God's wisdom there was only one who had the credentials to both accept the punishment for our sins and break sin's power.

Jesus took our sins and by his death met the requirement of the holy God, which means we can be exempted from eternal death which is the consequence of our failings. Peter puts it this way: "He himself bore our sins in his body on the tree, so that we might die to sins and live for righteousness; by his wounds you have been healed" (1 Peter 2:24). John adds, "He is the atoning sacrifice for our sins, and not only for ours but also for the sins of the whole world" (1 John 2:2).

Now what kind of God requires that? one might ask. The difficulty in making sense of this is not surprising, for it seems brutish, unfair, and downright ugly. The New Testament explanation is that the perfection of God's being requires that sin must be dealt with. Otherwise how do we explain the horrendous death he experienced? This sacrifice, which was central to his death, went beyond his dying being an example or a means to show us the depth of his love.

But now he [Christ] has appeared once for all at the end of the ages to do away with sin by the sacrifice of himself. Just as man is destined to die once, and after that to face judgment, so Christ was sacrificed once to take away the sins of many people; and he will appear a second time, not to bear sin, but to bring salvation to those who are waiting for him (Heb. 9:26-28).

What did Jesus' death and resurrection accomplish for humanity? First, he faced evil and won. Evil and death had such a hold on creation that to face it and bring it to the ground required divine activity. The very moment Jesus blurted out, "My God, why have you forsaken me?" he had been left by the Father to face evil alone. We have grown so accustomed to the trivializing of evil, such as in *Star Wars*, that we are prone to smirk at the very idea. However, the battle Christ waged on our behalf was rooted in the cosmic reality of good and evil with consequences playing themselves out in how we will live our eternal existence.

Along with overcoming evil, he brought a new ethic on living. In his Sermon on the Mount he reminds us what is good and what it means to live a good life. Paul advises Christians in Colosse, "Put to death, therefore, whatever belongs to your earthly nature: sexual immorality, impurity, lust, evil desires and greed, which is idolatry" (Col. 3:5). Good ethical standards aren't good just because they are admirable. They're good because they keep us from setting up other gods in place of Christ. This new ethic is not one of "pulling myself up by the bootstraps," and neither is it an abstract law calling for some unattainable goodness. The ethic is born in us by Christ, who gives power to live this new life, now and after we die.

Jesus' coming makes it clear that his vision for humanity goes beyond death. By his resurrection, death is accompanied by an actual expression of what we can expect we will be like after death and resurrection. We get a firsthand view of what we will be. Jesus didn't come back from the dead, eat with his disciples, say he was preparing a place for them, and tell them he was coming back unless that was his very plan. I may not trust some who promise they will return, but if there is anyone I can trust it is Jesus of Nazareth. His current work—as he promised—is to make ready a place that will be inhabited by those who are prepared to receive his life and live under his rule.

So what does this do for me, as I contemplate death? It breaks the fear of death. It lifts death's threat and creates a comfort zone so I can thoughtfully and with certitude anticipate that good life. It shatters my anxiety and apprehension about where I'll end up after death.

In giving me sight to see what is and will be, the resurrection assures me of a place. While church dogmas may seem cold and ancient, ivory tower arguments complex and removed, or experiences of others exaggerated or strange, the actual historical resurrection of Jesus of Nazareth guarantees me a place. What Jesus said overcomes ambiguity, uncertainty, and grayness.

Do not let your hearts be troubled. Trust in God; trust also in me. In my Father's house are many rooms; if it were not so, I would have told you. I am going there to prepare a place for you. And if I go and prepare a place for you, I will come back and take you to be with me that you also may be where I am. You know the way to the place where I am going (John 14:1-4).

We are also freed from guilt. In moments of reflection we know of our wrongs—destructive attitudes and habits, hurtful words and actions, wasted time, abuse of gifts. They ride like a dark cloud over our lives. Not only can they clog memories with unpleasantness, they disable us from healthy and productive lives. The failures of our unresolved past shape our sense of the future: "How can we anticipate the afterlife when memories continue to plague and burden us?" we ask.

The life of Jesus is the answer. The restoration of peace comes out of his life. The weight of guilt and deep regret are lifted by his life. This isn't to camouflage our past or pretend it never happened, rather it allows him to carry our guilt. The writer to the Hebrews puts it this way:

> But now he has appeared once for all at the end of the ages to do away with sin by the sacrifice of himself. Just as man is destined to die once, and after that to face judgment, so Christ was sacrificed once to take away the sins of many people; and he will appear a second time, not to bear sin, but to bring salvation to those who are waiting for him (Heb. 9:26-28).

But how does that help me in living today? Included in the benefit of Christ's resurrection is his empowerment. It's one thing to be freed from the fear of death and unburdened by guilt, but it is something else to be empowered to proceed.

The New Testament describes empowerment in four ways: *dunamis* (reserve power), *energeia* (applied power), *kratos* (mastery or control), and *ischus* (physical strength).

- *Dunamis* is latent power, reserved for when it is needed. God reserves for us what we need in times when we lack power. "Men of Israel, listen to this: Jesus of Nazareth was a man accredited by God to you by miracles, wonders and signs, which God did among you through him, as you yourselves know" (Acts 2:22).

150

- *Energeia* is the applied power that comes to us by his life merging with ours. "For the word of God is living and active. Sharper than any double-edged sword, it penetrates even to dividing soul and spirit, joints and marrow; it judges the thoughts and attitudes of the heart" (Heb. 4:12).
- *Kratos* is his continuing power that enables us to master our lives. "I pray also that the eyes of your heart may be enlightened in order that you may know the hope to which he has called you, the riches of his glorious inheritance in the saints, and his incomparably great power for us who believe. That power is like the working of his mighty strength" (Eph. 1:18-19).
- *Ischus* is stamina required to carry out daily work. "For some say, 'His letters are weighty and forceful.'" (2 Cor. 10:10).

What each of these has in common is the power of God's life, which in turn becomes ours by faith. Energy naturally diminishes with age and is finally frustrated by death. Christ's resurrection is the opposite; it counteracts that which robs us of energy and power. This is true in the moral and emotional compartments of living and finds its complete fulfillment in the resurrected life.

Christians in the early century, facing persecution and death, were assured by Peter of what was theirs in the moment of pain and death:

He has given us new birth into a living hope through the resurrection of Jesus Christ from the dead, and into an inheritance that can never perish, spoil or fade—kept in heaven for you, who through faith are shielded by God's power until the coming of the salvation that is ready to be revealed in the last time. In this you greatly rejoice, though now for a little

151

while you may have had to suffer grief in all kinds of trials (1 Peter 1:3-6).

How do I access this life? First, understand that heaven is real. The use of images of the afterlife—religious metaphors, fairy tales, and fiction—can tempt us to believe that this promise is just "pie in the sky." But metaphor and allegory help us discuss a world which, even though we can't see it, is real, prepared for those who love God.

Then receive the gift offered. Christ's gift must be received through faith. Faith in God's promise is not irrational, a leap in the dark, but belief based in trustworthy historical documents that give a clear account of Jesus. Our faith isn't myth, conjecture, or hypothesis. For two thousand years his message and life have lifted and transformed uncounted millions, setting them free from slavery, cultural bondage, and fear of life. It is this vision of life we are called to embrace.

We then live our lives with the promise that life forever is ours. Such hope transforms life today. Elevated from the miscues caused by cloudy thinking, I live today knowing that I live forever and what I do today has consequences for that future.

Eleven

WHAT ARE THE BENEFITS
OF LOOKING AT DEATH?

This heavenly city, while it sojourns on earth, calls citizens out
of all nations, and gathers together a society of pilgrims of all
languages, not scrupling about diversities in the manners, laws,
and institutions whereby earthly peace is secured and maintained, but recognizing that, however various they are, they all
tend to one and the same end of earthly peace.

Saint Augustine, *The City of God*

The underlying thesis of this book is how we can influence
our life after death. Life on earth is not, as some assume, just an
intermediate state, a time we endure to get into the next life. If
in believing that life continues after death we end up concluding that the joys and sufferings of this age are only transitory,
we overlook the overarching reality that life was originally
created for continuity, and it's in life that we determine the
nature of life beyond the grave. *Today matters!*

Death and taxes, it's been said, are unavoidable. Not quite
true. Payment of taxes can be negotiated and even delayed,
but death is irrevocable. Even so it seems that unless death is
staring us in the face we resort to all sorts of means to avoid it.
Alternatives to reality are convenient aids for avoidance. The
biblical literature calls them idols. Ancient civilizations and
cultures were rife with idols, representing every part of life.
However, one doesn't need to be part of an ancient or pagan
society to set up idols as a way of explaining away God.

Idols are anything that stand in place of one's trust and obedience to God. Children can become idols for parents if they become the focus and reason for life. Religion can also be an idol when the form of worship becomes what is worshipped. For some, being in love is a form of idol worship, as the person loved becomes the totality of the lover's existence. People working for justice can unwittingly make justice their object of worship instead of the God of justice. Idols blind us from seeing death as a part of life, which in turn keeps us from preparing for the afterlife.

The idol of freedom was first introduced to the human race with this lie: " 'You will not surely die . . . For God knows that when you eat of it your eyes will be opened, and you will be like God, knowing good and evil' " (Gen. 3:4-5). The lie was that if they but stood up to God they would be loosed from their limitations.

Another prevailing idol of our culture is hedonism, the drive to maximize pleasure. Though this form of idolatry is not unique to the Western world, the enormous rise of wealth provides time, opportunity, and creativity to feed the insatiable appetite for the "good life." A car advertisement alongside an American interstate reads, "Looks and money are everything." Hedonism holds us in the present without regard for what else in life is important.

An idol no less self-serving is utilitarianism: "the greatest good for the greatest number." So why is this idolatry? Its fault is the power that "the greatest number" has over the lesser. The Nazi thesis was, "Good is what benefits the Volk," meaning the greatest number. So those in minority or opposition or, worse, those whose bloodlines did not match what the leader defined as "the Volk," were sent off to the death camps.

One of the most common responses to the question of whether a person ends up in heaven is, "After all, I'm a good person." A 1996 poll by Barna Research Group found that 53 percent of Americans believe that all good people will go to heaven.[53] Most of us see ourselves as being reasonably good, at least in comparison to what we regard as "bad." When we consider reasons why God should promote us to heaven we fall back on an idol of relative morality, assuming, "I'm as good as the next guy." Our comparison implies an equation based on an average of goodness.

But the most common argument people make for why they'll live in heaven is the "God-who-is-love" idol. Ignoring other characteristics of God, we focus on this attribute, concluding that the only force influencing God's decisions is love, which by our definition means, "God wouldn't do something that in my view is unloving." Ignoring the larger and fuller statements about God, we fool ourselves with this stunted and yet widely revered idol of our times.

- *Idols distract us from seeing death through the lens of faith.* Since we carry over into the afterlife what we have become on earth, when we accept the false as true we deny ourselves the opportunity of building that which contributes to everlasting life. The more we allow idols to hold our focus, the more we fall prey to their false logic.
- *Idols misrepresent what is true.* As counterfeits, they resemble what's real. Rather than seeing them for what they are, we come to believe that they are the reality. For example, material benefits are a gift of God. But the distance from material well-being as a gift to an idol is not far. Wealth as a gift can distract one into believing that wealth itself is the reality.
- *Idols create pretense,* so that in pursuing a good cause we are distracted, believing that something like "dying for a cause" could be as vital as loving and serving God.

Subservience, even to something good, may conjure up expectation of being "worthy." As mighty as our efforts might be, the ultimate worthiness that gains us access to God's heaven is not the good we have done but the "good" Christ has done for us.

- *Idols create the illusion* that what they represent is of such value that not to give ourselves in their service seems out of the question. However, they not only represent what is false, they take over our lives so that truth is camouflaged, manipulated, and eventually denied. Our inability to track the good and true, and in this case to see the offer of life that Christ makes, is foiled by our inclination for the superficial or false.

If we serve anyone besides God we end up either ignoring the approach of death or, when that is no longer possible, choosing to believe that "God wouldn't deal me a bad hand," like a gambler placing his final chips in a wild hope to win the house. But we are not created to live that way. Our destiny isn't decided by one big crapshoot. Life does not need to be lived in ambivalence about what will be. We needn't assume that our only way out is a blind step into the unknown.

Moses was explicitly commanded not to have any physical representation of God, for as the people journeyed forward without a physical reminder, it pushed them instead to trust God for each day. The journey of faith is just that—faith, and faith alone. Our inclination to set up a facsimile of the original is not only distracting but misleading, inclining our minds to believe the imitation.

Seeing Beyond Idols to Creation

How can we see beyond idols so that death becomes an invitation to God's eternal life?

First we must understand the nature of creation. As I stand on our boat dock in the starlit night and do a visual sweep of the sky, I'm faced with one of two opposite impressions: I'm insignificant, or I'm important. As the *imago Dei* we stand within and on the edge of this vast enterprise, not as an unimportant cog in the wheel but as one made in the image of One who spoke this into being.

And what do I make of creation? Life, in all its forms, has intent. If I see the stars without reference to life and identity, my sense of creation's purpose and nature would be different and certainly much less. Creation expresses the nature of the creator so that all his handiwork gives worship and praise. If this was describing a scientist, politician, or artist it would be nothing more than self-promotion. But when we take off our shades of human limitation we see that creation honoring the creator makes sense.

We see that all of creation makes sense, filled with purpose and shaped by intent, the work of the gracious God we have come to know. Within that framework, death is not a concluding statement. And neither is the creator caught short by this aberration.

As a human I'm not the product of haphazard chances, but the result of the watchful eye and caring hand of the creator. I am not analogous to a mound or tree. As marvelous as is any part of creation, human life contains the imprint of God. As I see who I am as human, there is an unfolding vision of what God intends for me—for humanity—not only within this time-limited world but in the afterlife. The opening assignment to be God's helper in overseeing creation was never lifted. To

157

participate in the ongoing creation as stewards still stands as our assignment. Any denigration of humanity's significance or of one's personal worth and ability goes far beyond psychological damage, it flies in the face of the nature of life and denies the most fundamental statement of who we are. Once I understand who I am, I can see death for what it is.

However, we often fall into making one of two mistakes when dealing with death: underestimate it or overestimate it. We do the first when we sweeten its bitterness and pretend or assume that it is simply the natural wrapping-up of a good life or the merciful ending of a life of sorrow or sickness. As much as we try and dress it up, death is a violent end to life. In the beginning, death was not included. Death is a consequence. In fact, it's a punishment. The dying process is not more or less, depending on one's goodness or badness. We all die. Some earlier than others, but not always based on how one has lived. Death comes to us all, stripping life away from God's "good" creation. Never underestimate death. Death is the signal that judgment is just around the corner. There is no way to avoid facing the judgment seat of Christ, where we all will be judged, and on the basis of the judgment our eternal destiny defined.

The other danger is to give death a finality it doesn't have. Death wasn't included in our original genes. Eternity was. Unextinguished sorrow is not only a function of the loss of relationship but a failure to see that death is not the end. This is not to promote the often witless kinds of heaven-gazing in which we project feelings and images of a magical fantasy world. The gracious call of Christ is to see that death is an anomaly and not the end; death becomes a shadow. The fear it generates is broken by the sense of victory and we burst forth in the hymn, "Where, O death, is your victory? Where, O death, is your sting?" (1 Cor. 15:55).

Jesus, in restoring life to its creational intent, helps us see beyond our idols and fears. God's entry into human life came as the only way to restore the creation plan. The nature of God's holiness required that the sin debt of the human race be wiped out by payment. This is mysterious when viewed from my sense of justice. That God would accept a payment to offset the huge debt of human sin is, frankly, difficult to understand. However, this was God's choice.

This incarnation was more than God clothing himself with human skin. It was divinity becoming fully human so that Jesus was every bit as human as he was divine.

Benefits of the Death of Jesus

His death brought about a number of provisions. First, it provided a means by which we can be freed from the debt of sin and its consequences. As well, the evil of the cosmos is given notice of its coming defeat and obliteration. With respect to death, Christ faced it, died, and after three days provided the prototype of what our bodies and lives will be. It was resurrection, not resuscitation. Resurrection was the coming back into life in both the same and yet a changed state. It was the same in that he appeared to his friends as the same form. They recognized his speech and the scars in his hands. He ate and lived with them. But it was different in that it had a new atomic structure. Its constituents were not subject to death. The experience of death was bridged, so we in dying know that on the other side, after the transition, we will be fitted with a body that has *Eternal* stamped all over it.

We also need to see the human role in becoming a part of that rescue plan. There is debate among theologians as to our part in the future: to what degree does the human will come into play?

When God summoned Adam after the act of disobedience, Adam couldn't hide behind Eve or blame the serpent. Both he and Eve were, for the first time, self-conscious about their nakedness and quickly made clothes for themselves. These two were not animals but creatures imprinted by God. This image meant that they could be spoken to and were responsible. By this image we are not only given work, but we are held accountable and summoned into his presence. He called us at Calvary when he summoned all people in all time to hear his words of forgiveness. But he also calls us individually in our own lives to hear his words of life and to receive them in faith and with joy. Our lives matter. They are unique and within each life there are opportunities in which we can hear his voice.

Paul wrote to this effect: "For since the creation of the world God's invisible qualities—his eternal power and divine nature—have been clearly seen, being understood from what has been made, so that men are without excuse" (Rom. 1:20).

To live beyond the "sting" of death also calls me to see death as transition. To the Greeks "immortality of the soul" meant that the nonmaterial dimension of life continues forever in a disembodied form. For reincarnationists the soul goes through the cycle of becoming another creation in another life. Christian faith begins with the person—including the body and soul—as an original, without a prior life. Death, while bringing about the temporary cessation of the body, is overtaken in time and the body and soul are reunited after the resurrection, giving us the gift of everlasting life.

Biblical life is on a straight line of time, moving from the beginning in procreation to everlasting existence. Time is irreversible. I take all of me with me for I am my past, present, and future. I can't start over again after this life ends. The line of time doesn't allow us to return to Eden, to undo the past.

There is, however, the opportunity for a spiritual new birth during this life—when I receive the Spirit of God, who begins the process of recreating within me the life of Jesus. The remarkable story of the gospel is that I'm not bound by the past, even though it is my reality. With that in tow I bring my failure and discrepancies to Jesus, who accepts all of who I am and, in his power to forgive, lifts those burdens and debts and allows me to proceed in this new life into the future, to face death and know that in dying life is not ended. Then, rather than being the final statement, death becomes the new symbol of promise.

Twelve

WHAT IS OUR DESTINY?

> In any discussion of disappointment with God, heaven is the
> last word, the most important word of all. Only heaven will
> finally solve the problem of God's hiddenness. For the first
> time ever, human beings will be able to look upon God face
> to face. In the midst of his agony, Job somehow came up with
> faith to believe that "in my flesh I will see God; I myself will
> see him with my own eyes!" That prophecy will come true
> not just for Job but for us all.
>
> Philip Yancey, *Disappointment with God*

A friend, face pale and hands shaking, had just come from the doctor's. "What was in his report that has made you so upset?" I asked.

He turned away, his eyes moist and chin set to prevent trembling. He took a deep breath. "Brian, I've just been told I have cancer."

Death. Never had he faced his mortality in such a head-on way. He had been to countless funerals. He had sat with family and friends in many a hospital waiting room, encouraging those on the edge of death. Now it was his turn to look the possibility of illness and death in the face. And what he saw shook him to his very depths.

In another instance, a grand lady of faith looked kindly at me, and to my question of her feelings about dying said, "Brian, there is so much for me to look forward to: my husband, two children, and countless friends. And, of course, since I

162

haven't been there yet," she said, with a twinkle in her eye, "I do wonder. And at times I get a little anxious, but only for a minute until I remind myself that I'm really going home to the heavenly Father I've so wanted to see, face to face."

Then she shared her underlying mood. "You see, Brian, I'm also tired. At ninety-four, you just don't have the energy anymore. I've lived a full life, and I sometimes think today is as good as any day to go."

The settings, ages, moods, feelings are as many as there are people. The closer a friend, the more distressing the news is when we learn of their imminent death. The sudden pronouncement of our own mortality strikes us even harder.

There are two fears we face in living: failure to get what we hoped for out of this present life, and failure to get in the afterlife what we missed here. Youth is a moment in which the future is untarnished, filled with unhindered possibilities. We go off to college, scared and unsure of what we'll meet, but at the same time believing in our ability to meet the issues and build a life that has meaning along with the good times.

As we move through the eras of living, life's meaning gradually takes on different hues. In our optimistic and work-driven thirties and forties we pour energy into "making it." Then the big "5–0" arrives. All of a sudden our mortality looms unmistakably. For some, grandchildren remind us that life is not forever. Then retirement becomes not something down the road but just around the corner. If we haven't met our goals, middle age triggers a new awareness and we scramble to make up for lost time and lost investment.

But greater than that is the question, "Have I made a difference?" Some people are emotionally overloaded, believing that life has been unfair. Some disappointments spring from tragedies beyond our control. Or we author our own failure by unwise decisions and foolish, short-term actions.

Each of us at some point believes that "if only I had happiness, life would be as I expected." Suppose happiness is having all the money you want so you could do whatever you like. Would that be enough? Many who reach the pinnacle of financial success find that it never seems to be enough because the goal of life isn't as much in arriving as it is the process of getting there. Too often I meet people surrounded with all sorts of good things and ersatz happiness who recognize that in meeting their goals they haven't achieved what they wished.

C.S. Lewis, in *Till We Have Faces*, pictures expectations that miss the point:

"I have always . . . had a kind of longing for death."

"Ah, Psyche," I said, "have I made you so little happy as that?"

"No, no, no," she said. "You don't understand. Not that kind of longing. It was when I was happiest that I longed most. It was on happy days when we were up there on the hills, the three of us, with the wind and the sunshine. . . . And because it was so beautiful, it set me longing, always longing. . . . Everything seemed to be saying, Psyche come! But I couldn't (not yet) come and I didn't know where I was to come to. It almost hurt me. I felt like a bird in a cage when the other birds of its kind are flying home."[54]

When life seems best, when the opportunities outlast even the doing, we continue to look for something more.

The Old Testament "Song of Songs" is a script by a lover, making clear the lover's pursuit. Using sensuous words and images drawn from nature, it begins with the lover's wish for a kiss and ends with a profound desire for love's intimacy. She—Israel—sings out to her lover—God:

Under the apple tree I roused you;
there your mother conceived you,
there she who was in labor gave you birth.
Place me like a seal over your heart,
like a seal on your arm;
for love is as strong as death,
its jealousy unyielding as the grave.
It burns like blazing fire,
like a mighty flame.
Many waters cannot quench love;
rivers cannot wash it away.
If one were to give
all the wealth of his house for love,
it would be utterly scorned (Song of Songs 8:5-8).

Everlasting Life, Like Love, Is What We Seek.

We arrive at the end of life by way of paths we've chosen. As much as we might think life is haphazard, meaning it comes to us rather than by our choices, everlasting life is something we choose. The roads we choose make all the difference.

Which path will I take? I can try to go back to Eden, back to the place of innocence. In moments of guilt, when the pressures of mistakes and errant wanderings press themselves on memory, we want to go back and begin again. This illusory path of idealism is a mirage. I may pretend that what has happened never did. But this fantasy lasts no longer than a drug fix, then boom—back to reality. To search for Eden is not only futile but damaging because, by attempting to fix what is beyond repair, we delay doing what is right. To search for the tree of innocence is to look for what no longer exists.[55]

We wake up knowing we can't rescue those years of rebellion and foolishness. We can't go back and undo the divorce or

165

reclaim years lost from our children. The gospel is never about going back. The image of the new kingdom is, "To him who overcomes, I will give the right to eat from the tree of life, which is in the paradise of God" (Rev. 2:7). Moving forward in faith and Spirit empowerment, we know that in time we will eat of the good tree.

Another path I might take is that of unending reincarnations. For millions this is their choice, or at least the habit of their culture, from which they seem unable to break. For those whose present life is pleasant, filled with options and opportunities, this seems like a good option. But for those trapped in grinding poverty or under an oppressive regime it is anything but good. Their only hope is to live a good life and by so doing build karma, or credits of goodness, believed to influence the next cycle of life. This cycle of promise however, moving from one life to another, is endless and fatiguing.

There are two reasons this cycle is flawed. First is its vagueness and uncertainty. If one's future life is determined by how good one is in this one, what are the standards? How can one know with surety that if such and such is done now, in the next life one will be removed from the harshness and tedium of the present? The second is the loss of personal identity within endless life cycles. "Who am I?" I wonder. The ego of identity is an essential constituent of my being.

Time within the biblical record is quite unlike the cyclical vision of reincarnation. Time in the Genesis record is critical to the telling of the story and understanding that actions have consequences. The promise of death is a particular vision of the future. This time-path is a biblical understanding that the gift of life is sacred and not an illusion. For human life to be given the breath and image of God implies that life is not a transitory figment but has design and purpose.

There is another path many take, in which life revolves

166

around the self. Narcissism is an excessive interest in one's own sense of importance.

In Jean Paul Sartre's *Les Mouches*, Orestes, the hero, returns from Corinth to his home in Argus and is shocked by what he encounters. A dreadful guilt hangs over the city because of the killing of Agamemnon by his wife, Clytemnestra, and her lover, King Aegisthus. The citizens of Argus are ridden with guilt and fear over this killing, but when Orestes arrives home he resists it, asserting that he is free from it all for, "I am my freedom." He doesn't claim he has freedom, but that he is the embodiment of freedom. When citizens try to trap him in the guilt of the city he breaks away and escapes to the land of Nowhere, called Utopia, where he can begin again without the baggage of his previous broken world.

By defining freedom as himself and by dismissing the past, Orestes claims for himself omnipotence. The irony of his claims and of his trek to Nowhere is that his goal simply doesn't exist.[56]

But neither Orestes nor we can avoid our pasts. We may do it "our way," we may build bigger and better barns, as in one of Jesus' parables, but it all ends when dirt covers us. If the sum total of life is what we accumulate or become in our own eyes, we miss the nature of life while we live and, more tragically, goodness in the afterlife. I have never heard anyone muse at the end of life, "I wish I had made more money," or "If only I had spent more time working at the office." Instead we wish we had given more of living to what, in those fading hours, we realize it means to be human.

167

Attempts to Create a Heaven on Earth

In our post-modern world, we walk the path of trying to create heaven on earth. Twentieth-century secularization attempted to replicate heaven with a twist: "heaven happens here on earth in our time and on our terms." Rewarding good efforts, it tried to banish distinctions between rich and poor, well and sick, powerful and weak. Borrowing the biblical vision of the lion being led by the child, it promised paradise for all. The difference was that this "heaven on earth" was to be born out of only human efforts. Arising from nineteenth-century romanticism, it was shaped by a human inclination to do it on our own, to progress to the point that society becomes the heaven we imagine. Driven by the modern ideal of progress it saw a new heaven and new earth, not one in which God's righteousness reigns, but one where a humanized version of that is achieved.

Heaven on earth is a good thought, and those who promoted it as the fulfillment of the kingdom of Christ had good intentions. Filled with a sense of awe at the growing ability of science to produce more and more and better and better, the need for God to renew the heavens and earth seemed too much of a leap. Building competence along with centrally planned societies was the right way, so we thought. To organize and educate civilizations into living better is good. But in the end that too fails. As much as we saw in the early twentieth century the growing fulfillment of human goodness, it wasn't long before our benign ideal was blown apart by world wars, the use of technology to vaporize communities, and the genocides of tribal wars. These, along with new diseases, point out not that human efforts are wrong, or that the wonders of modern science are not appreciated, but that in walking this path of time we need to walk in hand with the creator.

Living in Two Worlds

We walk this path with an awareness that we are called to live in the world both as citizens and as aliens.

Intrinsic to our journey is our inbred restless spirit. Some call it dissatisfaction.[57] We are driven to improve what is, to begin what isn't, to grow a seed, to write on a blank sheet of paper, to climb a mountain just because it's there, to teach the young, to wrest from the jungles of Borneo a root to cure a disease. Such restlessness is a signal that we are bred from the beginnings of creation to push back the curtains of knowledge. In that we are citizens.

As followers of Christ we sing, "This Is Our Father's World." We were made for this world; it's naturally ours; we fit within its parameters. But there is no way to avoid living in tension. We rise in the morning facing the demands and assumptions of our world, regardless of our faith.

What is alien to Jesus' kingdom is what the New Testament calls worldliness—the pervasive dissonance of this age with God's world. As we are pulled by the concerns of this age, we are inclined to live in opposition to God and his creation. This generates a worldliness that disjoins God from nature and us from him. Worldliness, not the world, is what Christ's followers are alien to. Worldliness does not mean being a political leader, a scholar, creating wealth, or flying an airplane. These gifts become worldly only when used for ourselves: when our scholarship is used to prove others wrong so that in the end our name becomes revered; when our ability to grow ideas into companies to generate wealth is done so that personal wealth becomes the goal; when leading a nation or city becomes the aphrodisiac of personal power. That's what is "worldly."

Followers of Christ are paradoxically citizens of both worlds: the paradise of God's good creation—the earth—and the kingdom of heaven—which Jesus inaugurated and articulated. The two are not at odds. We are alien in that we are called to distance ourselves from that which robs us of the higher calling as followers of Jesus. Peter said as much: "I urge you, as aliens and strangers in the world, to abstain from sinful desires which war against your soul."

That is not to say one doesn't live in the world, as Peter makes clear: "Live such good lives among the pagans that, though they accuse you of doing wrong, they may see your good deeds and glorify God on the day he visits us" (1 Peter 2:12). The writer to the Hebrews, in listing the remarkable lives of heroic figures, calls them "aliens and strangers on earth" (Heb. 11:13), not because they had no linkage to their world, but rather because they were so far out in front of their peers and culture that in a sense they were strangers and even aliens, as if from a far-off country.

As we move forward, preparing for and expecting the great offering of everlasting life, there are times, places, and circumstances in which we live as if we were aliens, with a different code of ethics, seeing through different eyes. When the disciples were annoyed about people outside of their group casting out demons in Jesus' name, they were nonplussed by Jesus' response: "Anyone who gives you a cup of water in my name because you belong to Christ will certainly not lose his reward" (Mark 9:41). This acting within the guidelines of his new order anticipates the new order of heaven. Malcolm Muggeridge puts it this way: "The only ultimate disaster that can befall us, I have come to realize, is to feel ourselves to be at home here on earth. As long as we are aliens, we cannot forget our true homeland."[58]

The danger of feeling comfortable as a citizen of one's culture, which has been infected by the disease of rebellion and self-interest, is that we can be overtaken by its values. The essence of being both citizen and alien is to live in tension to such vulnerability. The longing for the goodness of heaven leads us up and out of the self-driven interests of much of what surrounds us.

To long for the good and best doesn't remove us from doing good in the world. Jesus, in his prayer for his disciples, made this clear. Jesus says to his Father, "I have given them your word and the world has hated them, for they are not of the world any more than I am of the world. My prayer is not that you take them out of the world but that you protect them from the evil one" (John 17:14-15). It's in this world that we find what we seek.

Heaven is what we choose; hell is also what we choose. Choosing often is not as clear-cut as whether to take the north- or southbound freeway. Choosing is part of a lifelong quest. Some gamble away opportunities in life, yet underneath there is that pull and desire to find God. The tragedy for so many is that when that quiet voice speaks in the early years of university, too often in an environment of cynicism and put-downs of matters spiritual, peer pressure becomes too great and the voice is silenced. When it is heard again, it may be amid the pressure of vocational success, and then too it is ignored. Again it may be heard in the midst of violating personal or public moral standards; it's muted again because its message is so inconvenient. Again and again it's silenced until we hear it no more. As time passes, and there is no more longing for God and heaven, one may wonder, was there no innate inclination? Yes, there was for us all, at some moment, in some place. If discouraged, it quietly went away. But never say the choice was never made.

Going home, our hope is rooted in what we believe God has made for us. Heaven is that home. God's creation, the earth as we know it, will be rid of undermining evil. The gloss and glitter that camouflage rebellion and self-interest are seen for what they are, and in the fires of God's presence, they are burned up:

171

"wood, hay stubble," all of it. Nothing is allowed into our ever-lasting home that is not good. God's re-creation of the heavens and earth, his resurrection of our lives and doing away with the Evil One provide us with a place we can finally call home.

C.S. Lewis puts it this way:

> Your soul has a curious shape because it is a hollow made to fit a particular swelling in the infinite contours of the Divine substance, or a key to unlock one of the doors in the house with many mansions. . . . Your place in heaven will seem to be made for you and you alone, because you were made for it—made for it stitch by stitch as a glove is made for a hand.[59]

In our everlasting home we'll retain our identities as persons. There is no fear of being lost in the crowd. There is a place with our name written on it. To a church in the Revelation the promise is this, "He who has an ear, let him hear . . . I will also give him a white stone with a new name written on it, known only to him who receives it" (Rev. 2: 17). There is something God considers unique in each of us. In our seeking, knocking, even blustery protests, he invites us to prepare to arrive at home expecting that our home is a gift unique and prepared with love and concern for those for whom he has died.

This path of life understands that life today is not just a tran-sition. As a child we sang, "This world is not my home, I'm just a-passing through." As engaging as this Sunday School song was, it is both a half-truth and a paradox. For years I lived with the sense that this world didn't matter; it was just a kind of launching pad for the next. What a mistake. It robbed me of seeing God's world as his gift.

The temporality of life doesn't mean that life here doesn't matter. The life we'll live in everlasting life is formed in this world. It mattered so much to God that his Son intermeshed his life with humanity; and if it matters to him it had better matter to us. Here we build the basis for our lives forever. In heaven we don't become different, that is, outside of the kind of person we are. Of course we are different in that our bodies and souls are no longer affected by evil or self-interest. But the building blocks of our lives are set in place here on planet Earth. Thus, this world matters, not only because it is God's creation and we've been called to serve, but because what we become here matters to who we'll be there. Thus that half-truth did enormous disservice.

The paradox is not that we live with one foot in each world, but that the two coexist, with heaven finally overtaking.

In walking with our creator we are empowered to do what is good. Everlasting life is promised as a gift, a gift that translates into eternal opportunities. The resurrection of Christ—the most important event in the calendar of human life—is our down payment on our future home. Evil forces determined to stop us dead in our tracks have been given their final destination. Peter says that at Christ's death he announced to Lucifer's angels that they were defeated (2 Peter 2:4).

The tragedy in life is that just when we reach our prime, aging becomes obvious: just when we reach the best of physical condition, when the mind is sharpest and most retentive, we begin the long slide of decay. My plans in youth didn't go the way I envisioned. The older I get the less energy I have to do what I wish. But all along, the resurrection sits as the opposite of my growing weakness. Rejecting the seeming inevitability of the unraveling of my prowess, I receive, not just for time but for eternity, the provision of unlimited life. The ending of this path is birth into a new life.

In these closing pages think about the heaven God has prepared for you, a place we don't end up at by chance or by assuming that God will make sure we end up there. Heaven is for those who trust in Christ for the resolution to our failure and rebellion. He is our "ticket" to heaven. It's not our good works, character, or upbringing that get us there. Heaven is for anyone—those who sorrow, those for whom life has been unfair and tragic, those seemingly untouched by tragedy and failure—for all of us who trust in the God who in coming made available this enormous gift of everlasting life.

The eternal world is now being prepared for you. It is God's promise to you. Whether you live in a palatial residence or an urban dump, you are promised a place of eternal goodness. It is not a foolish hope, no luck of the draw with God. Only your willingness to make his promise your received gift.

There is something you must do. This goodness doesn't fall out of the sky. Heaven is for those who seek it. "You will seek me and find me when you seek me with all your heart. I will be found by you" (Jer. 29:13-14). "Finding him is heaven. Seeking him is heaven's door. Not finding him is hell, and not seeking is the door to hell. The road to hell is *not* paved with good intentions but with no intentions, with 'I don't give a damn' or 'the hell with it.'"[60] We get to heaven by longing for it. Heaven is for those who want it, not for those who expect it as their right.

Jesus tells the story of a man having a visitor arrive at night and having no food to offer—an embarrassing circumstance in the Middle East. What does the host do? He goes next door and bangs on the neighbor's door. Only because of the insistence and boldness does the neighbor rouse from his bed and help out. Jesus, to ensure that the message hasn't fallen on undiscerning minds, explains, "Ask and it will be given to you; seek and you will find; knock and the door will be opened to you. For everyone who asks receives; he who seeks finds; and to him who knocks, the door will be opened" (Luke 11:9-10).

The choice is ours. We can choose life or death:

I have set before you life and death, blessings and curses. Now choose life, so that you and your children may live and that you may love the Lord your God, listen to his voice, and hold fast to him. For the Lord is your life, and he will give you many years in the land (Deut. 30:19-20).

What we want we find. Pursue heaven God's way and it will be yours.

In C.S. Lewis' *The Last Battle* in the Chronicles of Narnia, Lucy and her friends know it is time to leave Narnia and return home. Their heart is with the lion king, Aslan (the Christ figure), and, in their anticipation of having to leave, they feel sad. Aslan says to Lucy:

"You do not look so happy as I mean you to be."

Lucy said, "We're so afraid of being sent away, Aslan. And you have sent us back into our own world so often."

"No fear of that," said Aslan. "Have you not guessed?"

Their hearts leaped and a wild hope rose within them.

"There was a real railway accident," said Aslan softly. "Your father and mother and all of you are—as you used to call it in the Shadow-Lands—dead. The term is over; the holidays have begun. The dream is ended; this is the morning."

And as He spoke He no longer looked to them like a lion; but the things that began to happen after that were so great and beautiful that I cannot write them. And for us this is the end of all the stories, and we can most truly say that they all lived happily ever after. But for them it was only the beginning of the real story. All their life in this world and all their adventures in Narnia had only been the cover and the title page; now at last they were beginning Chapter One of the Great Story, which no one on earth has read, which goes on for ever, in which every chapter is better than the one before.[61]

ENDNOTES

1 www.deathclock.com
2 Near Death Experience Research Foundation Web Site: URL www.nderf.org. An interview conducted by Dr. Tricia McGill with Dr. Raymond Moody, professor of the Bigelow Chair of Consciousness Studies at the University of Nevada at Las Vegas.
3 Dr. Raymond Moody, "Life After Life" (Carmel, NY: *Guideposts*, 1978), pp. 15–16.
4 Elizabeth L. Hillstrom, *Testing the Spirits* (Downers Grove, il: InterVarsity Press, 1995), p. 83.
5 Gary Habermas and J. P. Moreland, *Beyond Death* (Wheaton, il: Crossway Books, 1998).
6 Habermas and Moreland, pp. 157–64.
7 Habermas and Moreland, p. 164.
8 Janice Mawhinney, "Death and Dying," *Toronto Star*, March 5, 2000.
9 Brendan I. Koerner, "Is There Life After Death?" *U.S. News and World Report*, online, March 31, 1997.
10 Hillstrom, p. 93.
11 Hillstrom, pp. 95–96.
12 Hillstrom, pp. 97–99.
13 Allan Kellehear, *Experiences Near Death* (New York: Oxford University Press, 1996), p. 42.
14 Hillstrom, pp. 87–88.

15 Habermas and Moreland, pp. 178–179.
16 Hillstrom, p. 92.
17 Roy W. Perrett, *Death and Immortality* (Boston: Martinus Nijholl Publishers, 1987), p. 78.
18 Perrett, p. 78.
19 Perrett, p. 78.
20 Perrett, p. 79.
21 Robert E. Neale, *The Art of Dying* (New York: Harper & Row Publishers, 1973), pp. 25–51.
22 John Lyden, *Enduring Issues in Religion* (Greenhaven Press, Inc., 1995), p. 228.
23 Robert E. Morey, *Reincarnation and Christianity* (Minneapolis, MN: Bethany House Publishers, 1980), p. 11.
24 Sylvia Cranston and Carey Williams, *A New Horizon in Science, Religion, and Society* (New York: Julian Press, 1984); Ian Stevenson, *Twenty Cases Suggestive of Reincarnation* (New York: American Society for Psychical Research, 1966); Mark Albrecht, "Reincarnation," *A Christian Critique of a New Age Doctrine* (Downers Grove, IL: InterVarsity Press, 1982); John Snyder, *Reincarnation vs. Resurrection* (Chicago: Moody Press, 1984).
25 From a poll on "Belief in Afterlife," taken by the Harris Poll on July 17–21, 1998, of 1,011 adults nationwide in the United States.
26 Tom Harpur, *Life After Death* (Toronto: McClelland and Stewart, Inc., 1991), pp. 105–10.
27 Paul Johnson, *The Quest for God* (New York: HarperCollins, 1996), p. 13.
28 Hans Küng, *Does God Exist?* (New York: Vintage Books, 1981), p. 639.

29 C.S. Lewis, *The Weight of Glory, A Chorus of Witnesses*, editors T.G. Long and C. Plantinga, Jr. (Grand Rapids, MI: Wm. B. Eerdmans Publishing Company, 1994), p. 85.

30 Ingmar Bergman, "The Seventh Seal," in *Four Screenplays of Ingmar Bergman*, translators L. Malmstrom and D. Kushner (New York: Simon & Schuster, 1960), p. 150.

31 Helmut Thielicke, *Living With Death* (Grand Rapids, MI: Wm. B. Eerdmans Publishing Company, 1983) p. 184.

32 Augustine, *Confession I.*

33 Alister E. McGrath, *Intellectuals Don't Need God* (Grand Rapids, MI: Zondervan Publishing Company, 1993) pp. 30–31.

34 Robert J. Banks and R. Paul Stevens, editors, *The Complete Book of Everyday Christianity* (Downers Grove, IL: InterVarsity Press, 1997), pp. 922–25; and Wayne Gruden, *Systematic Theology* (Grand Rapids, MI: Zondervan, 1994), pp. 472–82.

35 Often Bible translations do not consistently translate the words "soul" and "spirit" the same way but will sometimes substitute other words such as "heart," "mind," or "life."

36 For further reading see Steve Grenz, *Theology for the Community of God* (Nashville, TN: Broadman and Holman Publishers, 1994).

37 See Cullmann's analysis of the vision of the body and soul/spirit in Oscar Cullmann, *Immortality of the Soul or Resurrection of the Dead?* (London: The Epworth Press, 1958).

38 Cullmann, pp. 22–23.

39 Cullmann, p. 24.

40 Cullmann, p. 25.

41 Jeffrey Burton Russell, *A History of Heaven* (Princeton,
    NJ: Princeton University Press, 1997), p. 98.

42 "Both of the terms in the expression [*sōma* and *pneuma-
    tikon*] need careful definition. For Paul, the noun
    sōma (body) normally refers to the human person
    viewed as a whole, though with special emphasis on the
    corporeal and outward aspects of existence. The adjec-
    tive *pneumatikon* (spiritual) does not mean 'composed of
    spirit,' as though 'spirit' were some ethereal, heavenly
    substance. Rather, it signifies 'animated and guided
    by the spirit,' with *pneuma* (spirit) denoting either the
    Spirit of God or the human spirit as revitalized by the
    divine Spirit. The spiritual body, then, is the organ
    of the resurrected person's communication with the
    heavenly world. It is a form of embodiment that is
    fully responsive to the Christian's perfected spirit and
    perfectly adapted to its heavenly environment." Richard
    N. Longenecker, editor, *Life in the Face of Death* (Grand
    Rapids, MI: Wm. B. Eerdmans Publishing Company,
    1998), p. 153.

43 Longenecker, p.149.

44 Habermas and Moreland, *Beyond Death* (Wheaton, IL:
    Crossway Books, 1998), p. 281.

45 Philip Yancey, *Disappointment With God* (Grand Rapids,
    MI: Zondervan, 1988), pp. 245–46.

46 The results are based on an aggregated data set across
    Gallup Poll surveys conducted between 1992 and 1999,
    with a cumulative total of telephone interviews with
    40,610 adults.

47 Barna Research Group, March 18, 1996, poll. The
    survey found much disparity among Americans' views
    of hell. Three in ten adults (31%) see hell as an actual

location: "a place of physical torment where people may be sent." Slightly more adults, nearly four in ten (37%), say "hell is not a place, but it represents a state of permanent separation from the presence of God." Describing hell as merely a symbolic term, not referring to a physical place was true for two in ten Americans (19%). Ten percent of adults were undecided on their views of hell.

48 C.S. Lewis, *The Great Divorce* (New York: Macmillan Publishing Company, 1970).

49 C.S. Lewis, *The Problem of Pain* (London: Fount, 1977), pp. 101–102.

50 "The 'resurrection' of those who are to be raised and subsequently condemned will involve their appearance before God to receive their rightful judgment, presumably in some (undisclosed) bodily form that permits a continuity of personal identity. The silence of Paul and other New Testament writers about the nature of that embodiment of the wicked for judgment is in keeping with their concentration on the facts of humanity's universal accountability to God and the final state of the righteous, as well as their total silence on matters of physiology. Furthermore, if Paul does not regularly speak of a 'resurrection of judgment,' that is because 'resurrection' for him was not a purely neutral term signifying mere reanimation—merely 'coming to life again' after death—but a positive concept denoting the receipt of a permanent spiritual body like Christ's, with the concomitant enjoyment of eternal life." Richard N. Longenecker, editor, *Life in the Face of Death* (Grand Rapids, MI: Wm. B. Eerdmans Publishing Company, 1998), p. 151.

51 Habermas and Moreland, *Beyond Death* (Wheaton, IL: Crossway Books, 1998), pp. 302–19.

52 Quoted in Merrill C. Tenney, *The Reality of the Resurrection* (New York: Harper & Row Publishers, 1963), p. 92.

53 Barna Research Group, March 18, 1996, survey on Americans' views of heaven and hell.

54 C.S. Lewis, *Till We Have Faces* (New York: Harcourt, Brace, 1956), p. 74.

55 Peter J. Kreeft, *Heaven: The Heart's Deepest Longing* (San Francisco: Harper & Row Publishers, 1980), pp. 44–50.

56 Helmut Thielicke, *Living With Death* (Grand Rapids, MI: Wm. B. Eerdmans Publishing Company, 1982), p. 21.

57 Kreeft, p. 37.

58 Malcolm Muggeridge, *Jesus Rediscovered* (New York: Doubleday, 1979), p. 48.

59 Lewis, *The Problem of Pain*, pp. 117–118.

60 Kreeft, p. 26.

61 C.S. Lewis, *The Last Battle* (New York: Macmillan Publishing Company, 1956), pp. 173–74.

BRIAN C. STILLER serves as Global Ambassador for the World Evangelical Alliance and is president emeritus of Tyndale University College & Seminary, Toronto. His interest in the mysteries surrounding life after death pressed him to write *What Happens When I Die?*, a thoughtful book on biblical hope and its promise of life after death.

He is the author of a dozen books, including: *Preaching Parables to Post Moderns*, (Fortress Press); *You Never Know What You Have Till You Give It Away* (Castle Quay Books); *Jesus and Caesar – Christians in the Public Square* (Castle Quay Books); and *When Life Hurts - A Three-Fold Path to Healing*, (Harper Collins). He is founding editor of Faith Today.

Castle Quay Books

Other Castle Quay titles include:

Bent Hope (Tim Huff)
The Beautiful Disappointment (Colin McCartney)
The Cardboard Shack Beneath the Bridge (Tim Huff)
Certainty (Grant Richison)
The Chicago Healer (Paul Boge)
Dancing with Dynamite (Tim Huff)
Deciding to Know God in a Deeper Way (Sam Tita)
The Defilers (Deborah Gyapong)
Father to the Fatherless (Paul Boge)
I Sat Where They Sat (Arnold Bowler)
Jesus and Caesar (Brian Stiller)
Keep On Standing (Darlene Polachic)
The Leadership Edge (Elaine Stewart-Rhude)
Making Your Dreams Your Destiny (Judy Rushfeldt)
Mere Christianity (Michael Coren)
One Smooth Stone (Marcia Lee Laycock)
Red Letter Revolution (Colin McCartney)
Seven Angels for Seven Days (Angelina Fast-Vlaar)
Stop Preaching and Start Communicating (Tony Gentilucci)
Through Fire & Sea (Marilyn Meyers)
To My Family (Diane Roblin-Lee)
Vision that Works (David Collins)
Walking Towards Hope (Paul Boge)
The Way They Should Go (Kirsten Femson)
You Never Know What You Have Till You Give It Away (Brian Stiller)

BayRidge Books titles:

Counterfeit Code: Answering The Da Vinci Code Heresies (Jim Beverley)
More Faithful Than We Think (Lloyd Mackey)
Save My Children (Emily Wierenga)
Wars Are Never Enough: The Joao Matwawana Story (John F. Keith)

For more information and to explore the rest of our titles visit
www.castlequaybooks.com